SERIES EDITOR: MARTIN WINDR

MEN-AT-ARMS 346

THE PORTUGUESE ARMY OF THE NAPOLEONIC WARS (2)

TEXT BY
RENÉ CHARTRAND
COLOUR PLATES BY
BILL YOUNGHUSBAND

OSPREY
MILITARY

First published in 2000 by Osprey Publishing, Elms Court,
Chapel Way, Botley, Oxford OX2 9LP, United Kingdom

ISBN 1 85532 981 6

Editor: Martin Windrow
Design: Alan Hamp
Originated by Valhaven, Isleworth, UK
Printed in China through World Print Ltd

00 01 02 03 04 10 9 8 7 6 5 4 3 2 1

FOR A CATALOGUE OF ALL TITLES PUBLISHED BY OSPREY MILITARY
AND AVIATION PLEASE WRITE TO:

The Marketing Manager, Osprey Publishing Ltd, PO Box 140,
Wellingborough, Northants NN8 4ZA, United Kingdom
Email: info@ospreydirect.co.uk

The Marketing Manager, Osprey Direct USA, PO Box 130, Sterling Heights,
MI 48311-0310, USA
Email: info@ospreydirectusa.com

Or visit the Osprey website at:
www.ospreypublishing.com

Author's Note

Wellington's army in the Peninsular War was really an integrated
Anglo-Portuguese force, and the Portuguese element was more
important than is sometimes realised – between one-third and
one-half of the whole at any one time. The first title in this series,
MAA 343, covers Portugal's political and military situation at the
outbreak of war, Marshal Beresford's rebuilding of the Portuguese
army, the general staff and the line infantry. This second volume
covers the light troops, the Cazadores, the cavalry, the engineers
and the many smaller corps of the military and civil establishments,
as well as colours and standards. The forthcoming third volume,
MAA 356, will feature the artillery, militia, volunteers, Ordenanza,
offshore islands, colonies and the navy.

Based on Portuguese as well as newly discovered British
documents, it is hoped that this three-volume study will form
the most extensive source yet published in English on the
organisation and material culture of the Portuguese forces between
1793 and 1815.

With regards to the hues of colours described, blue was meant to
be a very dark blue; green was also dark. Scarlet or red ranged from
the 'brick red' of the common soldiers to a fine scarlet for officers.
White, especially for waistcoats and breeches, could also assume a
creamy colour.

The spelling of Portuguese follows the adaptations that have long
been prevalent in British and American military and historical
publications, in particular as expressed by Professor Sir Charles
Oman in his *History of the Peninsular War.*

Acknowledgements

The credit for much of the data presented in these volumes is due
to the excellent assistance given to the author by Dr Sergio Veludo
Coelho, military historian, and curator Dra Alexandra Anjos, of the
Museu Militar do Porto in the city of that name (Oporto). The
museum's director, Col Manuel Carvalho, gave every assistance, as
did the keeper of arms, Sgt Silva. Much kindness and patience was
shown by all staff to the author at a time when the museum was
undergoing restorations. I am also indebted to the Count of
Amarante and Marquis of Chaves, of the Friends of the Museum
Militar do Porto.

The author also gratefully acknowledges the kind assistance
given by William Y.Carman, Col Jacques Ostiguy, the Museu Militar
do Bussaco, the Anne S.K. Brown Military Collection at Providence
(USA), the Arquivo Historico Militar in Lisbon, and the Public
Records Office at Kew (UK).

Artist's Note

Readers may care to note that the original paintings from which the
colour plates in this book were prepared are available for private
sale. All reproduction copyright whatsoever is retained by the
Publishers. All enquiries should be addressed to:

Bill Younghusband,
Moorfield, Kilcolman West, Buttevant, Co.Cork, Eire

The Publishers regret that they can enter into no correspondence
upon this matter.

THE PORTUGUESE ARMY OF THE NAPOLEONIC WARS (2)

LIGHT TROOPS

This detail from a print of a street scene in Lisbon shows what appears to be an officer of the Cazadores in 1809 wearing a braided dolman and the 1806 shako with the plume on the left side.

ON 7 AUGUST 1796 a new all-arms light corps was raised at the behest of – and under the command of – General Pedro de Almeida, Marquis de Alorna. Entitled the **Legion of Light Troops (Legiao de Tropas Ligeras)**, it consisted of a battalion of eight companies of infantry; three squadrons of cavalry, each having two companies; and a battery of horse artillery armed with four six-pounders, having 56 men and 40 horses. The establishment totalled 1,339 men. Sometimes called the 'Experimental Legion', it was trained according to Alorna's adaptation of French tactical manuals.

The experiment, however, remained isolated. The Legion was somewhat resented by the more conservative elements in the army, and was treated as a separate entity; the tactical novelties which it practised – and which were being adopted in other armies – largely failed to spread to the rest of the army. Perhaps the only concession that might be ascribed to its avocation of light troops' tactics was the formation of a light infantry company in each infantry regiment. On 7 July 1803 the battery of artillery was incorporated into the Corte Artillery Regiment (see forthcoming third volume, MAA 356). The Legion was little affected by the 1806 regulations and remained a very distinct corps. In any event, the French soon marched in and the Legion of Light Troops was disbanded on 22 December 1807. The pro-French Alorna and some of his officers and men formed the Portuguese Legion (qv) in French pay.
Uniform See accompanying illustrations, and Plate A.

The Loyal Lusitanian Legion

The Legion was sponsored by Britain following an application by Portugal's ambassador, the Chevalier de Sousa, to raise it amongst Portuguese resident in Britain. On 29 July 1808 Lord Castlereagh granted approval. It was to have three chasseur (or light infantry) battalions of ten companies each, totaling 2,300 men, and a company of artillery with four light field guns and two howitzers. The Legion was commanded by Sir Robert Wilson; a few other officers were British, but most were Portuguese. Part of one battalion was raised from Portuguese in Britain, but the rest of the unit was recruited at Porto and Coimbra in Portugal during the late autumn of 1808. A corps of light cavalry of three squadrons was also added to the Legion's establishment at Porto, but in fact only a few despatch riders were enlisted. It is interesting to note that the Chevalier de Sousa, who represented Portugal's interest in the raising of the Legion, could not be persuaded 'to adopt the red clothing. He says that with that uniform every man would refuse to enlist'

(WO 6/164). In the event, as will be seen below, green was the colour adopted.

Following the withdrawal of Sir John Moore's British army from Spain via Corunna and Vigo in January 1809, the Loyal Lusitanian Legion found itself among the few regular troops guarding Portugal's northern provinces; indeed, it was probably the best equipped and officered unit in the area. Wilson, at his best when independent of senior commanders, left 700 men at the border fortress of Almeida and, with a mixed force of about 5,000 men – the Lusitanians acting as cadres to men who had only held a musket for a few weeks – advanced into French-occupied Spain. He passed Ciudad Rodrigo, attacking French outposts and convoys and spreading false rumours amongst the peasants. The startled French army commander, perplexed by these light troops harassing his rear, wondered in February if this was a 12,000-strong Anglo-Portuguese corps? However, as the French invaded Portugal from the north Wilson and his Legion were soon surrounded. It was only by scrambling through the mountains under conditions of great hardship that the Loyal Lusitanians escaped back to Portugal. Meanwhile, elements of the 2nd Battalion managed to retreat south following the capture of Braga and Porto in March 1809.

In May the 1st Battalion under LtCol Mayne fought a brilliant action at Alcantara against Marshal Victor. In August, during the Talavera campaign, Wilson was leading 300 men of his Legion together with the 2nd and 3rd Cazadores into northern Estramadura when he found himself slipping in behind the French army in the area of Bejar. At one point some scouts from his force were said to have got within nine miles of Madrid. While this was praised as very daring and of the 'greatest use' by many officers, it seems to have been a personal initiative of Wilson's which cannot have endeared him to Beresford or Wellington. Marshal Ney caught up with Wilson, whose force was humbled and scattered at Banos on 12 August. Wellington and Beresford were annoyed by this turn of events, and in October 1809 Wilson left in a huff for England, where he was later joined by Mayne.

The Loyal Lusitanian Legion might have lost its senior officers but its two battalions were still in Portugal. They were now to be incorporated into Beresford's Portuguese army and reorganised as standard battalions of ten companies. In late 1809 the 1st Battalion mustered 877 men and the 2nd had 749; but the Legion's training and discipline had evidently been neglected by Wilson. In January 1810 the Legion was inspected at Castelo Branco: the 1st Battalion had 792 officers and men, the 2nd had 1,146. General Hamilton, the inspecting officer, had 'expected a much more respectable Corps. The first is tolerable, the second bad – tho'

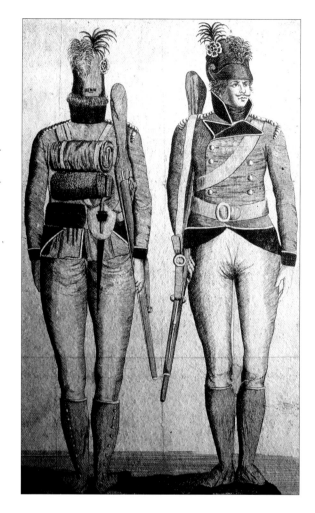

Infantrymen, Legion of Light Troops, c1796. Sky blue coatee with yellow-piped black collar, cuffs and lapels (open only at top) and turnbacks, brass buttons; yellow waistcoat and breeches, black gaiters; black hat or cap with yellow cords and black plume. (Museu Militar do Porto)

dressed as light troops they have not practiced the movements, indeed I think they are much behind in discipline'. Lieutenant-Colonel Grant, commanding the 1st Battalion, was now the senior officer. The officers and men were considered good material, but until they could be properly trained in light infantry manoeuvres they were really troops of the line. The emphasis was thus placed on training.

Both battalions, totalling 1,646 all ranks, were deployed but not heavily engaged at Bussaco on 27 September 1810. After retreating to the Lines of Torres Vedras the Legion formed part of Gen Campbell's 6th Division. The unit had never been a true legionary corps, and had now become simply two light infantry battalions within the Portuguese army.

The 1st Battalion, 572 strong under LtCol Edward Hackshaw, was part of Beresford's army at the hard-fought battle of Albuera on 16 May 1811. It was heavily engaged and its gallantry helped win the day, but at a loss of 171 officers and men. The 2nd Battalion was also much below strength. Beresford felt that more battalions of light troops were needed in the Portuguese army, and Wellington agreed. To fill this need, Beresford called on the Loyal Lusitanian Legion for a final service. On 20 April 1811 the raising of six new Cazadores battalions was authorised. By the same decree the Loyal Lusitanian Legion was disbanded so that its officers and men could be used to form the 7th, 8th and 9th Cazadores battalions (qv).

Uniform See accompanying illustrations and Plate A.

CAZADORES

In the autumn of 1808 the Portuguese army found itself totally without regular light infantry units. The Legion of Light Troops (qv), disbanded in late December 1807, could not be re-formed as most of its men had been used to form the light infantry battalion in the French army's Portuguese Legion (qv). Light infantry would therefore have to be organised, equipped, armed, clothed and trained from scratch. Consequently the Portuguese general staff ordered the creation of a new light infantry arm to be called 'Cazadores', the Portuguese word for hunters or chasseurs. It was hoped that with rigorous training in modern light infantry tactics the Cazadores would become elite units within the army – a hope that was to be vindicated.

The first six battalions of Cazadores were authorised to be raised on 14 October 1808. From 23 November 1809, each battalion was to have a staff of 23 officers and men consisting of: one lieutenant-colonel, one major, one adjutant, one quartermaster, one paymaster, one adjutant-sergeant, one quartermaster sergeant, one chaplain, one surgeon, two assistant surgeons, one artisan, one gunsmith, one bugle-major, one bandmaster and eight bandsmen. Each company had one captain, one lieutenant, two sub-lieutenants or ensigns, one first sergeant, two second sergeants, one third sergeant, eight corporals, eight second or lance-corporals, two drummers, one bugler and 96 private soldiers, giving a total company establishment of 123 officers and men. Each battalion had four ordinary Cazadores companies and one elite Tiradores ('sharp-shooters') company. The five companies and battalion staff came to a total establishment of 628 officers and men.

Back view of a gunner of the Legion of Light Troops, c1800. (Anne S.K. Brown Military Collection, Brown University)

5

The officers and battalion cadres were organised as far as was possible during the next two months. As in the line infantry, each Cazadores battalion was attached to a town or city. The 1st Battalion was assigned Castelo de Vide, the 2nd Moura, the 3rd Vila Real, the 4th Viseu, the 5th Campo Maior and the 6th Porto.

On 15 December 1808 the order to draft the men was issued, and it was quickly obeyed; many came from local volunteers. The 1st Battalion was formed with the Portalegre Volunteers Regiment in Alentejo province; the 2nd with part of the Transtagana Legion (Regiment of the Honoured Volunteers of Beja) in Alentejo; the 3rd was raised at Vila Real in Tras-os-Montes, the 4th at Viseu in Beira, the 5th with part of the Transtagana Legion at Campo Maior in Tras os Montes, and the 6th in Minho. All these were provinces on the north-eastern border with Spain, where the French were expected to attack next; men with a thorough knowledge of these rough mountainous areas were especially sought-after. Indeed, most Portuguese Cazadores were mountaineers and men from small farms in the hills, familiar with hunting habits and experienced in handling guns since childhood. The state of the new battalions and where they were assembled as compiled at the end of December 1808 (PRO, WO 1/232) is given here as **Table A**.

Some 2,419 men had joined the Cazadores within two weeks, but there were barely enough arms for half of them, and only part of one regiment reported uniforms in wear. During 1809 the number of Cazadores climbed to about '3,000 chasseurs', and stayed at that level for a couple of years. In April 1810 there were a total of 3,018, of whom 2,366 were 'present and fit for duty' (PRO, WO 1/244). This was below the establishment strength, which is not surprising. However, it must be remembered that there were also the two stronger battalions of the Loyal Lusitanian Legion, which were considered part of the light troops. The Cazadores battalions were trained according to British light infantry manuals which were translated into Portuguese by William Warre, Marshal Beresford's ADC.

The good services of the Cazadores, who quickly made themselves a reputation as daring elite troops, and the increased need for light infantry, brought about a consolidation and an increase in the establishment of such units. On 20 April 1811 a decree created six additional battalions of Cazadores, to have the same establishment as previously. As we have seen, the Loyal Lusitanian Legion was disbanded to form

Officer, Light Cavalry of the Legion of Light Troops, c1807. The cavalry had sky blue light dragoon-style dolmans with black collar and pointed cuffs, yellow cords, small brass buttons; white and sky blue breeches, black boots; black leather Tarleton-style helmet with fur crest and white feather (green from 1806); and sky blue housings edged with yellow. Buglers and trumpeters had red coatees or dolmans, the other details being similar to the men's uniforms. Officers had gold lace and buttons and a red sash with silver fringes. (Print after William Bradford)

Table A: Cazadores Battalions, December 1808				
Battalion	men	arms	uniforms	location
1st	339	250	-	Castelo Branco
2nd	321	260	-	Moura
3rd	239	185	203	Trancoso
4th	614	-	-	Penamacor
5th	120	95	-	Campo Maior
6th	646	500	-	Vila Real

Infantry fusilier's coatee, Loyal Lusitanian Legion, c1808-10. This is all green with white cords and lace and white metal buttons. The basic coatee is original but has had various restorations over the last hundred years. In the back view note the false turnbacks, which are simply a triangle of lace on the skirt. (Museu Militar do Porto)

three battalions: the 7th formed in Guarda, the 8th in Trancoso and the 9th at Lamego. The recruiting area of these three battalions was the province of Beira. The 10th was raised in Aveiro from volunteers in the Porto District. The 11th was raised at Feira, and was said to be 'composed of fine healthy lads from the northern provinces', who 'were in as fine order as any troops in the world' when they passed through Coimbra in March 1812. The 12th Battalion was raised at Ponte de Lima with recruits from the province of Minho. By early 1812 the distribution of the battalions was reported as listed in **Table B** (PRO, WO 1/401). The province was the general area for recruiting the conscripts, who were first drafted by the Ordenanza and trained by the affiliated militia regiment. The quarters were where the units had their depots.

Table B: Cazadores Battalions, early 1812		
Battalion	province	quarters
1st	Estramadura	Lisbon
2nd	Algarve	Mertola
3rd	Beira	Aguiar da Beira
4th	Estramadura	Tomar
5th	Alentejo	Campo Maior
6th	Minho	Penafiel
7th	Estramadura	Aldeia Gavinha
8th	Beira	Idanha
9th	Minho	Braga
10th	Porto	Soure
11th	Beira	Guarda
12th	Tras os Montes	Braganza

The Cazadores went on to earn ever greater distinction. In the final years of the war, in 1813 and 1814, the 2nd, 4th, 5th, 7th and 9th battalions fought on the Nivelle and Nive rivers, at Bayonne and Toulouse. By then they were considered elite light troops by both the British and the French. For instance, Lt Woodberry noted that the 2nd Cazadores were on picket duty guarding the general headquarters in January 1814, showing Wellington's great confidence in these troops. When the battalions returned from France to Portugal they were all assigned new HQ and depot locations. The 1st was assigned Portalegre, the 2nd Tomar, the 3rd Vila Real, the 4th Penamacor, the 5th Miranda do Douro, the 6th Penafiel, the 7th Guarda, the 8th Trancoso, the 9th Sao Pedro do Sul, the 10th Aveiro, the 11th Feira, and the 12th Ponte de Lima.

Cazadores uniforms

The dress of the Cazadores battalions was decreed in the regulations of 11 November 1808. The cloth for the uniforms did not come from

England; it was a locally produced woollen country cloth called 'zaragoza', of a medium to dark brown hue, fairly rough but very sturdy – an ideal material both in colour and in texture for skirmishers. The 3rd Cazadores appear to have been the first to report having some uniforms, but the 1st was also clothed at about the same time at Portalegre thanks to a gift of uniforms and equipment from its wealthy lieutenant-colonel. At Bussaco, where all six Cazadores units were deployed, the French noted 'several Portuguese battalions dressed in brown' fighting them stubbornly. It should be noted that the Cazadores' uniforms were made in Portugal.

All battalions had a dark brown jacket, with collars and cuffs of the battalion colours as listed in **Table C**.

The jacket was trimmed with yellow cords, green piping and round yellow buttons. The jacket of the ordinary Cazador appears to have had three rows of buttons with yellow cord braiding on the chest, and green piping edging the collar, cuffs and shoulder straps. The elite companies of Tiradores had in addition green fringes to the ends of their shoulder straps. The waistcoat and pantaloons were dark brown or white according to the season, and the greatcoat was to be the same as for the line infantry. The short gaiters were black.

The first shako was the 1806 'barretina' as worn by the line infantry. It had a brass bugle horn badge, the battalion number stamped in the brass lower band, and green cords. On the left side the ordinary Cazadores had a green plume while the Tiradores had a black plume. The shako changed in about 1809-10 to the British 'stovepipe' light infantry model with brass bugle horn badge, battalion numeral, and green or black plume in front.

The NCOs were distinguished by yellow silk cords as well as the rank badges of the 1806 regulations. For drummers, buglers and fifers, see Plate B.

Major John Scott Lillie, 7th Cazadores Battalion, c1811-14. The portrait is very dark, but many details can be distinguished. The jacket is dark brown with a black collar, yellow pointed cuffs edged with two gold lace stripes, black buttons and black cords braided across the chest; he wears dark brown pantaloons and a crimson and gold hussar-style barrel sash. The shako on the table at left is black with brass or gilt chinscales, a gilt stringed bugle horn badge with the Roman numeral 'VII' below, green cords and a green plume. The black crossbelt has a silver whistle, and he holds a sabre with a Mameluke hilt. The Portuguese and British medals and orders were painted in later and include the British Military General Service, first awarded in 1848. (National Army Museum, London, 58364)

Charge of Cazadores, 1811-14. *Azujelo* by Jorge Colaço done at the end of the last century to commemorate the battle of Bussaco. (Bussaco Palace)

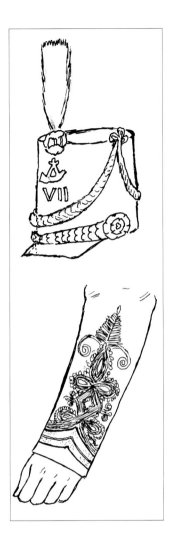

Detail of the shako after Major Lillie's portrait; and reconstruction of a Cazadore major's cuff and sleeve lace and embroidery, c1814.

Officers and cadets were to be distinguished by gold cords on their jackets. Epaulettes and rank badges for all ranks were to be according to the uniform regulations of 19 May 1806 (see first volume, MAA 343).

The yellow and gold cap cords cannot have been universally displayed; they were hardly a discreet feature for men acting as skirmishers, and in those ruinous times for Portugal the gold cords would undoubtedly have been an unbearable expense for most officers. No doubt there were complaints; and on 11 July 1809 the colour of the cords and buttons was allowed to be black for all ranks.

Perhaps as early as 1809-10, some Cazadores sergeants started wearing sashes and black chevrons, no doubt in imitation of British sergeants. The sashes were forbidden by Marshal Beresford on 2 April 1810; but in his order of 24 March 1813 he eventually concurred that chevrons with three or four bars of black lace would 'continue' to be worn by Cazadores.

In 1811, as noted above, the number of units was doubled. By a General Order of 30 July 1811, the uniform of all 12 battalions was ordered to be as follows: dark brown jacket with pointed cuffs and collar of the facing colour as listed in **Table D**. The jackets were to be trimmed with black cords and black round buttons. There were three rows of buttons on the front, with cords braiding the chest, black lace edging the collar and cuffs; and dark brown shoulder straps edged black, with black fringes. The waistcoat and pantaloons were to be dark brown. This remained the official dress for the rest of the Peninsular War; see illustrations and Plates B and C (though it may have been simplified during the war for some Cazadores – see Plate C). The shako remained cylindrical until about 1815 when it assumed a bell-top shape.

For officers, the portrait of Major Lillie of the 7th Cazadores shows the battalion's black collar and yellow cuffs on a jacket which is covered with black cords held by three rows of black buttons. It also shows two gold laces above his cuffs; and there are no epaulettes on his shoulders. As Lillie left the Portuguese service in April 1814, this would seem to indicate that the rank badges specified on 24 October 1815 (given below) might already have been adopted unofficially for some years by some officers – as we have seen, this was already the case regarding the rank badges of sergeants.

The rank badge situation was officially solved by the order of 24 October 1815 which brought in a system of laces to denote the rank of officers and of chevrons (now gold or yellow instead of black) for sergeants and corporals, as follows:

Lieutenant-colonel Two wide gold laces edging the cuffs.
Major One wide gold lace edged with a gold cord.
Captain One wide gold lace only.

Table C: Battalion distinctions, November 1808

Battalion	collar	cuffs
1st	dark brown	sky blue
2nd	dark brown	scarlet
3rd	dark brown	yellow
4th	sky blue	sky blue
5rd	scarlet	scarlet
6th	yellow	yellow

Table D: Battalion distinctions, July 1811

Battalion	collar	cuffs
1st	black	sky blue
2nd	black	scarlet
3rd	black	black
4th	sky blue	sky blue
5rd	scarlet	scarlet
6th	yellow	yellow
7th	black	yellow
8th	sky blue	black
9th	scarlet	black
10th	yellow	black
11th	sky blue	scarlet
12th	scarlet	sky blue

Lieutenant Two gold cords.

Ensign One gold cord.

Sergeant-adjutant Four gold lace chevrons on the right sleeve with a gold bugle horn badge at the centre of the top chevron.

Quartermaster-sergeant Four gold lace chevrons on the left sleeve with a gold bugle horn badge at the centre of the top chevron.

First sergeant Four gold lace chevrons on the right sleeve.

Second sergeant Three gold lace chevrons on the right sleeve.

Third Sergeant Three gold lace chevrons on the left sleeve.

Artificer and *bugle-major* Three gold lace chevrons on the right sleeve.

Corporal Two yellow lace chevrons on the right sleeve.

Lance-corporal One yellow lace chevron on the right sleeve.

Finally, the unit chaplains supposedly wore their religious garb, but it was different in the Cazadores battalions. Captain Kinkaid of the 95th Rifles described the chaplain of 'our two Cazadore regiments' – the 1st and 3rd Cazadores in the Light Division – as 'a short stout old fellow, with a snuff-coloured (brown) coat buttoned up to the throat' wearing a 'tall cocked hat' and 'mounted on his bay pony in his Portuguese saddle which is boarded up like a bucket (the shape of his seat and thighs)'.

Arms and accoutrements

Officers were to be armed with a sabre. All NCOs and soldiers were armed with muskets and bayonets. All soldiers, drummers, fifers and buglers were also to have a short sword. Drum-majors, drummers, fifers and buglers were to have a pistol instead of a musket. In practice, the short swords and pistols do not appear to have been found for all, nor worn by some or all for very long. With only 1,290 firearms, presumably of all descriptions, for 2,416 Cazadores in December 1808, the priority was to arm everyone with good weapons as soon as possible. This was done in 1809 thanks to the large supplies of British muskets flowing into Portugal. The armament became the standard India Pattern musket with bayonet. British light infantrymen were not armed with sabres and there is no evidence that any were sent for the Cazadores. From 1809, the Cazadores were armed like British soldiers.

Accoutrements were to be black with bayonet and sabre frogs for the waistbelt and a shoulder cartridge box belt for those carrying muskets. Drum-majors, drummers, fifers and buglers were to have a pistol holster instead of a bayonet frog. Again, due to lack of arms, these instructions may have remained largely on paper. In practice, black British accoutrements would have been used from 1809 for the British muskets with which they came. The brass belt-plates appear to have

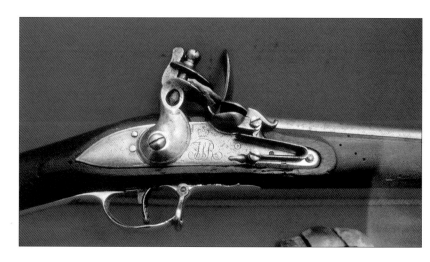

Lock on a British India Pattern musket marked with Prince Regent Joao's cipher 'JPR', indicating that this weapon was refurbished or reassembled at the Lisbon Royal Arsenal between 1808 and 1816. (Museu Militar do Bussaco)

been left plain. Black rifle accoutrements were issued to the men using rifles from August 1810.

It was originally intended to have rifles for some or all the Cazadores but these were not available in 1808-09. The 2,000 Baker rifles, complete with sword bayonets and accoutrements, which were ordered from England by Beresford and Wellington in June 1809 arrived in Portugal during the spring of 1810. The six battalions then had about 3,000 effective men. Part of each battalion was issued with these rifles in the late summer. D'Urban noted in his journal for 6-7 August: 'The Marshal (Beresford) gives them Rifles to complete. The other Chasseurs are attached to Brigades under British Officers… and will therefore improve rapidly. 200 Rifles ordered also for each of the Chasseurs 1st, 4th, 6th' battalions. There were thus about 200 riflemen per battalion – perhaps somewhat less in the additional battalions raised in 1811, as there is no evidence of further rifles being sent to the Portuguese army. The only addition would have been the maximum of 120 rifles from the disbanded Loyal Lusitanian Legion, giving a total of some 2,100 rifles. Assuming the first six battalions kept 200 rifles each, this left the last six battalions with 150 rifles each – still a respectable proportion of riflemen in any army.

Royal Volunteers of the Prince

While not involved in the Peninsular War, this sizeable regular corps consisting mostly of Cazadores should be mentioned, if only to avoid confusion. The Voluntarios Reales do Principe was ordered raised on 15 May 1815. It consisted of four battalions of Cazadores numbered one to four totalling 4,830 men, two companies of artillery and 800 cavalry. The units were divided into two brigades with staff officers. Formed by drawing volunteers from other units in the army, this corps embarked for Brazil in early 1816. Renamed 'of the King' following the death of Queen Maria I, the corps took part in the capture of Montevideo in 1817.
Uniform See illustration.

CAVALRY

The Portuguese cavalry originated in 1640 when a number of permanent companies were mustered as part of the new regular army raised by King Joao IV. They were organised into regiments from 1707, but all were disbanded and totally reorganised from 1715. Regiments of dragoons were added to the heavy cavalry units from the 1730s, and the Braganza Light Cavalry in 1754; the dragoon regiments were Olivenza, Evora, Chaves and Miranda. The Count de Lippe reorganised and augmented the cavalry to 12 regiments which could best be defined as medium cavalry. Although some of the regiments officially kept their titles as dragoons until 1806, they were in fact all similar from the 1760s and were routinely designated as 'cavalry' in almost every document. The arms, equipment and uniform were similar for all regiments. There was no light cavalry such as hussars or light dragoons.

Cavalry regiments, as organised under Count Lippe's 1762 instructions, consisted of eight companies, each with a captain, a

Shako, 6th Cazadores Battalion. Black felt and leather, brass numeral and bugle horn badge, blue and red cockade, green pompon. The badges are of a latter date than the Napoleonic era but generally similar to earlier ones. (Museu Militar do Porto)

lieutenant, a cornet, five NCOs, a trumpeter, a farrier and 30 troopers, making about 300 officers and men per regiment. This was increased in the 1790s and early 1800s to 470 all ranks. Before the French invasion of 1807 regiments had, on paper, 58 troopers per company with a suitable number of good horses. This was the theoretical strength determined by the army HQ at Lisbon; the reality in the various garrisons was very different. The actual strength of cavalry regiments was much lower than establishment, perhaps as low as half in some cases. There were not enough horses even for these reduced numbers of troopers, and the training appears to have been fairly abysmal.

Tactically, the Portuguese cavalry were not really heavy cavalry, nor were they trained to be dragoons, and they were certainly not light cavalry. Here lay the root of the problem. The general staff never really made up its mind as to what role the cavalry was to fulfil on the battlefield. As a result, the mounted arm was not divided to perform the various tactical functions incumbent on cavalry of the Napoleonic period, as was the case in most other armies. The only tangible effort in that direction was the creation of the squadrons of light cavalry in the 1796 Legion of Light Troops (qv). Even the reforms of 1806 did not really address the problem other than to reorganise that arm into something like medium cavalry. There were no provisions for true shock heavy cavalry, nor were more light cavalry created.

It could be said that Portugal was not quite a 'horse country' like England, France or Spain in terms of breeding a plentiful variety of mounts. The typical horse was a good and sturdy animal, but somewhat too small for heavy cavalry and a bit too slow for light cavalry. Most crucial was the fact that the country could never produce enough horses nor forage for a large cavalry establishment. It was thus the weakest arm

Cazadores, Royal Volunteers of the Prince, 1815-16: detail from a print after J.B.Debret. The uniform of the four Cazadores battalions was inspired by those in Portugal but made somewhat simpler, without black cords. The jacket was brown with a single row of black buttons in front and black turnbacks, green wings, the collar and cuffs of various battalion facings (yellow is shown in this print); white pantaloons, black gaiters, shako with brass bugle badge and green plume, and black accoutrements. Note the white bugle ornaments painted on the black British 'Trotter' knapsacks with mess tins in white covers and white straps; the canteens painted green with black bugle ornaments; and white haversacks. The men are shown armed with muskets.
(continued opposite)

Cavalry uniform, 1806-10. The uniform shown is after the plates in the May 1806 regulations. It remained largely the same during the Peninsular War except for the replacement of the helmet by the shako in 1810-11.

Watercolours in the Arquivo Historico Militar show some detail differences from Debret's renderings made in Brazil. The former show the Cazadores' brown jackets with brown cord across the chest and black turnbacks; the 'stovepipe' shakos have brownish cords, a green plume and brass stringed bugle badge with the number. The 1st Bn have brown collar and sky blue cuffs; the 2nd, sky blue collar and brown cuffs; the 3rd, brown collar and scarlet cuffs; and the 4th, black collar and scarlet cuffs. The cavalry are shown with the 1806 pattern blue coatee with white collar, cuffs, piping and turnbacks, brass buttons; and bell-topped shako with yellow top band, oval brass badge and red plume. The artillery have the blue coatee with black collar and cuffs, yellow piping and possibly turnbacks, brass buttons, and black shako plume.

of service in the army. All this explains in large part the lacklustre role it played during the Peninsular War. Following the French occupation at the end of 1807, Marshal Junot considered it next to useless and disbanded it. He correctly believed that the best elements, which included the better light cavalrymen from Alorna's Legion of Light Troops, could make useful light cavalry, and formed them into two mounted chasseur regiments in the new French Portuguese Legion (qv).

During the second half of 1808 the Portuguese cavalrymen gathered and spontaneously reformed their old regiments, although severely short of horses, arms and uniforms. The cavalry's situation was compiled as shown in **Table E** at the end of 1808 (PRO, WO 1/232).

Thus, in December 1808, the cavalry had 3,641 men but only 629 uniforms and 2,617 horses. Arms were not listed, but a 'great want of harness, carbines, pistols and swords' was noted.

In 1809 Marshal Beresford reorganised the Portuguese cavalry to have an establishment of 595 officers, NCOs and men per regiment, giving a total of 7,140. Each regiment had a staff and four squadrons, with two companies per squadron. There were no elite companies. The

Table E: Cavalry regimental strengths, late 1808

Regiment	men	uniforms	horses	location
1st	344	149	233	Lisbon
2nd	88	-	1	Beja
3rd	325	160	364	Evora
4th	410	100	252	Lisbon
5th	284	-	65	Evora
6th	300	-	300	Chaves
7th	317	100	225	Lisbon
8th	218	20	36	Elvas
9th	300	-	300	Chaves
10th	226	100	179	Santarem
11th	427	-	377	Almeida
12th	452	-	285	Braganza

Officer, 1st Alcantara Cavalry Regiment, 1808-09: print after William Bradford. Bradford is the only source to show the coloured front edging this wide – other paintings show it as normal piping. The helmet plate has been omitted. Alcantara wore blue with white collar, cuffs, piping and turnbacks and gold buttons.

regimental staff had one colonel, one lieutenant-colonel, one major, one adjutant (a senior NCO), one quartermaster, one brigade sergeant, one quartermaster sergeant, four standard bearers, one chaplain, one surgeon-major, two assistant surgeons, one picador, one trumpet-major, one saddler, one gunsmith for woodwork and one for ironwork. Each of the eight companies had one captain, one lieutenant, one ensign, three sergeants, four corporals, four lance corporals, one trumpeter, one farrier and 56 troopers. Each regiment was supposed to be 'in every respect, similar to the British cavalry, and manoeuvre upon the same principles', according to Halliday.

Sufficient mounts were now even harder to find due to the ruinous French invasions. Part of the country, especially the centre and the north where most of the horses were bred, was devastated, and thousands of farms had been ruined and abandoned during 1808-11. At the same time, great quantities of forage had to be found for the British cavalry as well as the Portuguese. Priority was given to the large British cavalry contingent, which was already deployed in the

Table F: Cavalry regiments, 1811-12

Regiment	area	condition	serving
1st	Alcantara	completed	in the field
2nd	Moura	dismounted	garrison
3rd	Olivenza	dismounted	garrison
4th	Mecklemburg	completed	in the field
5th	Evora	completed	in the field
6th	Braganza	part mounted	recruiting
7th	Lisbon	completed	in the field
8th	Elvas	completed	in the field
9th	Chaves	dismounted	garrison
10th	Santarem	completed	in the field
11th	Almeida	part mounted	in the field
12th	Miranda	dismounted	garrison

Table G: Regimental distribution, early 1812

Regiment	province	depot
1st	Estramadura	Lisbon
2nd	Alentejo	Evora
3rd	Beira	Aviero
4th	Estramadura	Torres Novas
5th	Alentejo	Evora
6th	Minho	Aveiro
7th	Estramadura	Lisbon
8th	Beira	Castelo Branco
9th	Tras os Montes	Chaves
10th	Estramadura	Torres Novas
11th	Beira	Castelo Branco
12th	Tras os Montes	Chaves

field and vital to the war effort. In any event, what horses were found for the Portuguese cavalry came mostly from the provinces of Beira and Tras os Montes, and were considered to be small by British observers. With such difficulties in obtaining mounts, some of the Portuguese cavalry regiments were often short of recruits – who must not have been sought too earnestly at times.

From 1811 to 1812 the condition of the cavalry regiments was generally as indicated in **Table F**. As can be seen, there were really too many regiments for the numbers of horses available. Another factor was the shortage of well-trained and experienced Portuguese cavalry officers and NCOs; British officers had been attached to make some regiments effective. Only six regiments were truly operational in the field, two were 'part mounted', and the rest were simply used as dismounted garrison troops.

By early 1812 the distribution of the regiments to provinces and depots was reported as shown in **Table G** (PRO, WO 1/401).

Of the regiments in the field, the 1st and 7th formed a brigade under BrigGen Otway, and 'distinguished itself very much' against French cavalry near Badajos in 1811 and at Salamanca on 22 July 1812. Its tactical role was clearly defined as light dragoons, and the 1st/7th Brigade was attached to the British Light Cavalry Division. The 4th and 10th were also brigaded as light cavalry. The 1st and 11th 'behaved nobly' at Salamanca under the command of Benjamin D'Urban, but were scattered and put to flight at an affair against French

Portuguese cavalry charging French dragoons. This detail from a contemporary print shows the cavalrymen wearing shakos with the oval plate.
(Museu Militar do Porto)

cavalry at Majahonda near Madrid on 11 August. The 5th and 8th formed a brigade under BrigGen Maddon, and served with the Spanish forces in Estramadura during 1811-12, where they seem to have been employed as light and medium cavalry.

As can be seen, Portuguese cavalry sometimes wanted confidence and might suddenly scatter, but they also gave some good service, such as the 1st and 11th at Salamanca. Still, as D'Urban noted after seeing them charge 'like British dragoons' at Salamanca, only to vanish a few days later before 'French helmets', they were an 'uncertain sort of fighting people'.

In early 1813 it was decided to mount only the 1st, 4th, 6th, 11th and 12th regiments and to leave the rest as dismounted units in garrisons. Regiments frequently mustered less than 300 men from an official establishment of 595. At the end of the war in 1814 the 12 regiments were reduced to an establishment of 6,372 men and 5,220 horses, although it must have been much less in reality. In 1816 the establishment went back to Peninsular War levels.

Cavalry uniforms

The Portuguese cavalry adopted blue uniforms from 1762. In the 1790s the regiments all wore a blue coat without lapels and with the regimental distinctions shown in **Table H**.

The various manuscripts occasionally show variations from the above colours: Mecklemburg is shown with green facings in 1797, and Braganza with sky blue; Chaves is shown with crimson facings in 1791, scarlet in 1792 and brown in 1797; and Almeida is shown with green facings in 1797. All regiments had white waistcoats and buff breeches. The lace edging the hats was of the button colour; the capes were blue, and housings were blue edged with the button colour. Information on the uniforms of trumpeters before 1806 is very scant; they seem to have had the same uniform as the men with extra lace, but there is too little data to draw conclusions.

In about 1801 the crested leather helmet started to appear in the cavalry, probably as a result of a recommendation by the Duque de Lafoes, who believed that they offered much better protection than hats. The Braganza Regiment is known to have adopted such a headdress at about that time. A surviving helmet was described as being of black reinforced leather with a fur crest on top, a plume socket on the left, a yellow metal band bearing the name of the regiment and a small oval brass plate with a monogram bearing the letters 'IML'. Most of the regiments continued to wear bicorn hats with white or yellow lace edging, although the new fashion of leaving them plain was making inroads. On 28 January 1805 the officers of the Caes Cavalry Regiment were allowed to wear hats without lace.

Officer, 9th Cavalry Regiment, c1815-20. The dress shown is generally similar to that used during the later part of the Peninsular War except that the shako is more elaborate, with a drooping plume. Its bottom band bears the inscription 'Chaves', which was the 9th's area. The standard lace epaulettes were adopted from about 1812. The 9th Cavalry had a blue coatee with yellow collar, cuffs, piping and turnbacks, gold buttons and epaulettes. (Museu Militar do Porto)

The officers had the same basic uniform but made of better materials. The epaulettes and lace were gold or silver depending on the regimental button colour. The sashes were red with silver fringes.

The Portuguese cavalry streamlined its uniforms from 19 May 1806, adopting a blue single-breasted coatee with the regimental distinctions listed in **Table I**. The turnbacks were the colour of the piping with a small blue triangle as ornament. The pockets were vertical with a slant. The colour of the piping and turnbacks worn by a regiment corresponded to one of the three divisions between which they were divided: red for the Southern, white for the Centre, and yellow for the Northern. The shoulder straps consisted of narrow brass scales with narrow wing-like extensions at the top of each shoulder. Buttons were plain brass for the men and gilded for officers.

The jackets were worn with blue, white or grey breeches, black boots, and white buff leather gauntlet gloves; black leather sabretaches with a brass badge bearing the arms of Portugal, and white accoutrements. The headgear was a black leather helmet with a brass oval front plate with the regimental number and narrow brass bands edging the black leather turban, black hair crest, red plume above the blue and red cockade on left side, and brass chinscales. Instead of a cape, an ample blue greatcoat with a shoulder cape was adopted, with collar and cuffs of the regimental facing colour. Housings were to be blue edged with yellow.

From 1810-11, uniforms were sent from England to some or all regiments; e.g., the 5th and the 8th Cavalry in 1811. The range of the clothing sent is given in the November 1811 invoice for the uniforms of the 5th Cavalry: the sergeant-major, 24 sergeants, 24 corporals, 24 lance-corporals and 467 privates each had a dress jacket, an undress jacket, a pair of overalls, a watering cap, a shako (see below), a pair of 'boots with fixed spurs', a stock and clasp, and each sergeant had a sash (PRO, WO 1/849). It is interesting to note that breeches are

Table H: Regimental distinctions, 1790s

Regiment	collar	cuffs	turnbacks	buttons
Alcantara	pink	pink	pink	white
Moura	yellow	yellow	yellow	white
Olivenza	blue	blue	blue	white
Mecklemburg	sky blue	sky blue	sky blue	white
Evora	white	white	white	yellow
Braganza	blue	blue	blue	yellow
Caes	crimson	crimson	crimson	white
Elvas	scarlet	scarlet	scarlet	yellow
Chaves	scarlet	scarlet	scarlet	yellow
Castelo Branco	scarlet	scarlet	scarlet	white
Almeida	scarlet	scarlet	scarlet	yellow
Miranda	scarlet	scarlet	scarlet	scarlet

Table I: Regimental facings, May 1806

Regiment	collar & cuffs	piping
1st (Alcantara)	white	white
2nd (Moura)	white	scarlet
3rd (Olivenza)	white	yellow
4th (Mecklemburg)	scarlet	white
5th (Evora)	scarlet	scarlet
6th (Braganza)	scarlet	yellow
7th (Lisbon)	yellow	white
8th (Elvas)	yellow	scarlet
9th (Chaves)	yellow	yellow
10th (Santarem)	sky blue	white
11th (Almeida)	sky blue	scarlet
12th (Miranda)	sky blue	yellow

Marks on M1796 British heavy cavalry carbine used by Portuguese cavalry. (Museu Militar do Porto)

no longer issued to this regiment serving in the field with Wellington's army. The undress jacket, overalls and watering cap were probably of the same general patterns as used in the British cavalry: blue round jacket with collar and cuffs of the facing colour, blue or grey overalls strapped with leather, and blue watering cap with facing-colour trim.

At about that time the cavalry adopted the British black bell-topped light dragoon shako, with black bands and a triangular black leather plate (point up) with brass regimental number, brass chinscales, blue and red cockade, and red plume. As early as May 1810 there were instructions to 'ship some caps (shakos) provided by direction of Major White for the use of the 10th Regiment of Portuguese Cavalry'. In November 1811 an invoice mentions that shakos were sent to the 5th Cavalry (PRO, T 28/9 and WO 1/849).

A watercolour by Denis Dighton shows an officer wearing the blue coatee with scarlet collar, cuffs and turnbacks, white piping, gold buttons, the British bell-topped shako, gold British-type fringed epaulettes and crimson sash. The overalls are also blue with leather strapping. The facings shown correspond to the 5th Cavalry, but the shako is shown with the numeral '10' in gilt (see Plate E). As the facing colours listed above were the official ones, it seems that Dighton may have been working from various notes sent to him by his brother in Portugal. Other variations can also be seen in Portuguese prints of the early 19th century (see illustrations), but they do confirm the shako having replaced the leather helmet. For trumpeters, see Plate D.

Very badly armed and equipped at the outset of the 1808 uprising, the cavalry desperately needed re-equipping. Marshal Beresford requested from England, in June 1809, some 5,000 saddles, bridles and saddlebags, 6,000 carbines, 6,000 swords, and 4,000 pairs of pistols. These supplies started reaching the Portuguese forces at the end of the year (PRO, WO 1/239 and 884). Accoutrements were also sent, such as '1,000 light dragoon carbine pouches and belts' shipped in June 1810 (PRO, WO 1/844). Some '4,000 sets of horse shoes of the same pattern as that of the Royal Horse Artillery' were shipped in March 1811 (PRO, T 28/8). Later, in February 1813, Wellington requested a further '3,000 carbines for (Portuguese) cavalry with accoutrements complete', and '1,000 saddles, bridles and horse accoutrements complete' to replace worn out and lost items (PRO, WO 1/257). Arms of this period preserved in the Porto Military Museum show that pattern 1796 light cavalry and 1796 heavy cavalry sabres were sent, as were 1796 heavy cavalry carbines and cavalry pistols (see illustration).

The great fortress at the seacoast town of Peniche. Built from the 16th century and massively transformed into a Vauban-type fortress from the latter part of the 17th century, it is a fine example of the works made by Portuguese military engineers. The French had left a negligible garrison which was quickly overcome in July 1808. Thereafter the fortress was put to use by Marshal Beresford as the Portuguese army's first central depot for training infantry recruits.

18

SPECIALIST CORPS

Royal Corps of Engineers

Portuguese military engineers built substantial works not only in their country but also in their colonies of Brazil, Angola, Mozambique and posts in India. From the late 16th century military engineering was supervised by an Engineer-Major of the Kingdom (Engenheiro-Mor do Reino) who headed this distinct professional department within the armed forces. This senior officer and his staff were in charge of the building and upkeep of fortifications in the country. He was assisted in each province by an Engineer-Major (e.g, Engenheiro-Mor da Provincia do Minho) and his own staff of engineers. The number of engineers in Portugal hovered around a hundred or so at the turn of the century. Overseas, there were nine in Brazil, one in India and one in Angola.

At the time of the Peninsular War the most formidable coastal works were at Peniche and the fortresses near Lisbon. The frontier with Spain had two massive fortresses: Almeida to the north, and the mighty fortress of Elvas facing southern Spain. Captain Sherer noted that the latter had 'the protection of an impregnable out-fort (La Lippe) which is looked upon as a chef d'oeuvre of skill in fortification'.

Following the ousting of the French, the engineers were regrouped and reorganised. On 4 November 1808 the Royal Corps of Engineers – Real Corpo de Engenheiros – was created under a commandant, the first of whom was Marechal de Campo Antas dc Machado, succeeded by LtGen Diaz Azevedo on 16 December 1810. The corps was described by Halliday as having 'many officers of ability and intelligence', and consisted in 1812 of eight colonels, 13 lieutenant-colonels, 27 majors, 22 captains, 11 first lieutenants and 11 second lieutenants. They adapted quite well from their previous role of permanent fortification engineers to that of field engineers, and carried out an enormous task alongside the British Royal Engineers in building the Lines of Torres Vedras in 1809-10. Indeed, it is not generally known that a Portuguese engineer, Maj Neves Costas, drew the initial plan for the lines. Only three Portuguese engineers were directly under the orders of the British Royal Engineer, Capt John Jones, who supervised the work, but another 40 Portuguese engineer officers were involved in various aspects during the construction of the lines. At least ten Portuguese engineer officers later served in the field with the Portuguese component of Wellington's army through Spain and into southern France. The engineers also supervised and provided the cadre staff officers for the Royal

Obidos is one of many Portuguese towns fortified in the Middle Ages which were still useful as bases for raiding parties during the French invasions. From Obidos, Lt Fenwick of the British 3rd Foot (the Buffs), who was detached to the Portuguese service, led daring militiamen in some 20 raids against the French from late 1808.

Major José Joaquim Talaia, Royal Corps of Engineers, c1796. The uniform would have been blue with black velvet collar and cuffs, gold buttons, gold and black epaulettes. Major Talaia's outstanding defence of Campo Maior in 1811 made him a national hero. (Print after portrait)

Plan of the fortress of Vila Vizosa. Elaborate bastions and redans are built around the old 16th-century castle, whose two turrets at opposite corners can be seen. Such improvements were made to many castles all over Portugal. (Museu Militar do Porto)

Academy of Fortification, the Telegraph Corps (qv) and the Battalion of Artificers (qv).

Uniform Until the early 1790s, sky blue coat, black collar and cuffs, yellow turnbacks; buff waistcoat and breeches, gold buttons and lace. This changed in about 1796 to a blue coat with black collar and cuffs, blue lapels, scarlet turnbacks, blue waistcoat and breeches and silver buttons. In about 1801 the lapels disappeared and the dress coat became single-breasted with gold laced buttonholes, the undress coat being plain (see illustrations). For the 1806-15 uniform, see illustration and Plate F.

Royal Arsenal

From 1640 an arsenal was set up in Lisbon for making arms and ammunition; it was destroyed twice, first by fire in 1726 and then by the disastrous earthquake of 1755 which destroyed much of the city. Ordered reconstructed in 1760, a large new facility was opened in 1764 under the name of Royal Arsenal of the Army. Its foundry specialised in casting brass ordnance well into the 19th century, and it also manufactured muskets for the army. The arsenal had a large staff of specialist officers, artisans and workers. At the beginning of the 19th century there were 33 officers, 50 masters and specialists supervising over 2,000 workers of various sorts. The Artificer Company (qv) also served there from 1803. Until the end of 1807 the muskets made there were generally like the British models but with barrel bands. There was also an experimental model which looked like a Long Land Pattern with an inside lock, made at the Royal Arsenal in 1792 for the Freire Regiment. The arsenal soon went back into production following the expulsion of the French in 1808, concentrating on casting canons and howitzers. In time many 'rare and curious' military objects were kept there and, in 1851, the facility was converted into the Military Museum of Lisbon. Today it also houses the Army Historical Archives.

Uniform See Plate F.

Artificer Company (Comphana de Artifices) Raised on 7 August 1803, this was based at the Royal Arsenal in Lisbon. Its men were to ensure uniformity in the manufacture of various artillery equipments. They were under the direction of engineer officers for certain technical work. The company was also attached to the Corte (or 1st) Artillery Regiment and served as its artificers and pontoneers.

Uniform See Plate F.

Battalion of Artificers (Batalhao de Artifices)

This was the Corps of Engineers' contingent of artisans enlisted to serve in the field; their officers were thus detached from the Engineers. It was ordered raised on 12 February 1812, but actual formation really began on 24 October when Beresford gave further orders to provincial governors, instructing them to send drafted militiamen to form the battalion. Preference was to be given to volunteers skilled in various trades such as carpenters, tinsmiths, blacksmiths, tanners, locksmiths, miners, etc. The pontoneers and miners of the artillery regiment were transferred to the new battalion. It was commanded by a major with a staff consisting of one first lieutenant as adjutant, one first lieutenant as quartermaster-paymaster, and a quartermaster sergeant. Each of the three companies had a captain, a first lieutenant, a second lieutenant, four first sergeants, five second sergeants, one third sergeant, ten corporals, ten lance-corporals, 40 privates and one drummer. The men were divided into squads of pioneers, artificers, miners, pontoneers and sappers.

The battalion marched into Spain in 1813 and was at the siege of San Sebastian. The establishment was altered on 18 October 1813 to two companies of artificers and a company of pontoneers. The pontoneer company had the same strength as before but each of the two artificer companies was augmented to two second lieutenants and 100 privates, giving a total of 348 officers and men. The battalion was kept at the same establishment at the end of the war.

Uniform Blue coatee with blue collar and cuffs, black lapels, scarlet turnbacks and piping, brass buttons; white or blue pantaloons, black gaiters; shako with brass plate and band, black plume. The black lapels may have been discontinued in about 1814 and the plume changed to black and white.

Telegraph Corps (Corpo Telegraphico)

The 1810-11 campaign in Portugal is probably the first in which optical telegraphs – a kind of simple 'semaphore' tower – were used on a large scale to transmit messages. In late 1809 the Anglo-Portuguese army command decided to set up a network of lines of telegraphs across parts of the country in the interests of speeding the transmission of messages. Corps of Engineers BrigGen Pedro Folque went about this task with diligence and enthusiasm. Four lines were set up in the spring of 1810, with Lisbon as their focal point: between Oitavos and Lisbon (four posts), which rapidly reported whatever shipping appeared at the mouth of the Tagus; between Almeida, the great fortress on the northern frontier, and Lisbon (16 posts); between Barquinha and Abrantes (two posts); and between Santarem, which connected with the Almeida–Lisbon line, and Elvas, the large fortress on the eastern border (six posts). This last line was not really operational until early 1812, and was then extended up to near Badajos in Spain.

(The telegraph network along the Lines of Torres Vedras – five stations, the main one at Sobral – from October 1810 to April 1811 was not manned by the corps but by British Royal Navy officers and men, as it was in frequent

Captain, Royal Corps of Engineers, dress uniform, c1802. Blue coat, black velvet collar and cuffs, scarlet turnbacks, gold buttons and lace, gold lace epaulette on a blue strap; crimson sash with silver tassels, white breeches, black boots; black bicorn with gold cockade loop and white plume; gilt-hilted sword with crimson sword knot and silver tassels. (Anne S.K.Brown Military Collection, Brown University)

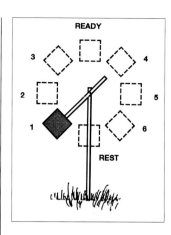

READY

3 4
2 5
1 6

REST

Probable appearance of a Portuguese Telegraph Corps signal mast, c1810-15. Devised by Gen Folque, each station was designed to be as simple as possible to set up for rapid transmission. It consisted of a mast with a movable arm with a three-foot-square panel at the end. The panel was moved to pass signals according to a simple message code, its six possible positions combining to signify numbers which corresponded to hundreds of words or parts of phrases from Folque's code book: e.g. '351 = battle won by...'.

communication with the fleet. They used naval-style masts to hoist a system of ball signals.)

The telegraph lines consisted of a series of small posts built on prominent hills, each manned by a few soldiers. The intervals between stations averaged about 20-25km (12-15 miles), although some were closer and others further apart depending on the terrain. The speed of transmissions is not known; but it was now possible to send a message from Lisbon to Almeida, at the very northern end of the country, in an unheard-of matter of hours, rather than several days by courier. Secrecy was not sought, but it was obscure enough for the French, who never bothered to find out about it and used nothing like it themselves in the Peninsula.

To operate the telegraphs the Corpo Telegraphico was created by order of 5 March 1810. It recruited among retired or invalid soldiers able to read and write who volunteered for further service, and a few also came from line regiments. They were supervised by seven engineer officers. The corps had a director general (Gen Folque), six officers as first adjutants to the director general, and three as second adjutants; the enlisted men consisted of 17 first corporals, 28 second corporals and 64 private soldiers – a total of 119 officers and men. Most telegraph posts on the long Lisbon–Almeida line had three to five men each, and the Barquinha–Abrantes chain two to four men; but the Santarem–Elvas line had only one man per post. If the enemy approached they were to promptly destroy their post and retreat rather than put up a fight – such posts could easily be rebuilt.

Wellington, who was always seeking the latest news and put much value on intelligence, appreciated the telegraph, and it continued to be used in his army in Spain and southern France during the later phases of the Peninsular War. Edmund Wheatley of the King's German Legion noted in January 1814 that a 'telegraphic communication is adopted when the army is in winter quarters', which was set up near the mayor's house of Guethary where Wellington had his HQ. In 1814 Wellington organised a small telegraph section of one officer, one NCO and three enlisted men for each of the divisional HQs in his army; it would seem that the Portuguese component of the army provided these services. After the Peninsular War the Telegraph Corps continued to exist as a distinct unit until incorporated into the Battalion of Artificers as its telegraph company on 30 December 1830.
Uniform See Plate G.

Military Academies

The training of officers for the Portuguese forces followed the traditional patterns of European armies. The great majority of aspiring officers, often from noble families, were at an early age appointed cadets in a regiment where a father or an uncle was already a commissioned officer. While the basic military and academic education gleaned by cadets from older officers and the regimental chaplain was more or less adequate for ordinary duties, there were practically no facilities for higher learning in military sciences. The best and brightest might get ahead on their own by acquiring and studying specialised books.

Some military schools had been organised in the fortresses of Elvas and Almeida from 1732 to train prospective engineers. In 1761 the

College of Nobles was created, and was 'previous to the war, a most excellent institution' which gave some military instruction to young noblemen until 1807; thereafter, wrote Halliday, 'its halls are now deserted, and the building is made a barrack for a militia regiment'. This college, however, was not a totally military school.

Such an institution opened in Lisbon during January 1790: the Royal Academy of Fortification, Artillery and Design (Academia Real de Fortificaciao, Artilharia e Desenho) for engineer cadets. It became the Army School in 1837, and is today the Military Academy of Portugal, the institution of higher military learning. Following Portugal's defeat in the 'War of the Oranges' against Spain, one of the reasons identified for the failure of the Portuguese forces was the lack of formal schooling of aspiring officers. A large, well-run military college was the obvious answer, but little was done. In 1803 the small Feitoria College opened in Lisbon, initially intended for cadets of the Corte (later 1st) Artillery Regiment; its cadets were sons of officers.

These institutions were shut down from late 1807 soon after the French marched into Lisbon; but after they were expelled formal officer training was restored. In 1812 the British ambassador Sir Charles Stuart reported that the 'Military College for the education of officers, which admits 65 pupils, is now established at Peynas, and is to be regulated according to the system which has succeeded in other countries. This school will be divided into Departments for the education of officers of the line, the artillery and the engineers, and removed to Thomar' (PRO, WO 1/401). This reorganisation occurred in 1813, and the Feitora College became the Royal Military College. There were also military schools in the offshore islands and in Brazil (see forthcoming third volume, MAA 356).

Uniform Cadets in regiments wore their regimental uniforms with a gold lace edging each cuff and a gold star on each shoulder. Those at the Military Academy and the Feitora College probably wore the engineers' and the Corte (1st) Artillery Regiment's dress respectively.

Corps and staff officers' uniform, 1806-15. These figures from the May 1806 regulations show the uniform details of the specialist corps such as the Engineers and General Staff officers. The civil departments had essentially the same dress but usually in sky blue and without the sash, since they were not commissioned combatant officers. Treasury and Commissariat eventually had dark blue with gold epaulettes but without sashes or plumes. Civil officers carried the inoffensive smallsword rather than the sabre.

Guides of the Army (Guias do Exercito) There is little information on the Guides, who appear to have been a company raised under the 1806 reforms. It apparently evolved into a group of information officers attached to the general staff of the army, possibly assisted by enlisted men. It seems to have been disbanded in 1814, but a company of guides is again part of the 1816 organisation.

Uniform Blue coat, green collar, cuffs, piping and turnbacks, gold buttons; bicorn hat laced gold with mixed blue, green and gold tassels, white and green plume.

Garrison Staff (Estado Mayor de Praza) Fortresses and fortified towns had a staff of garrison officers who were usually concerned with routine administration and maintenance and the billeting of troops passing through. Their usual ranks were governor, major and 'ajudante' (adjutant, but acting as ADC). At the major fortresses of Abrantes, Almeida, Elvas, Peniche, Setubal, Belem, St Julio de Barra, Lagos and Cascaes the governors were senior generals assisted by a major and an adjutant. Somewhat lesser fortresses such as Estremoz had governors with the rank of brigadier-general. Most other fortified places had governors with the rank of colonel or lieutenant-colonel assisted by an adjutant. There were 45 fortresses and towns with 83 garrison staff officers in November 1812. Nine were senior generals, five were brigadier-generals and the remainder were colonels, lieutenant-colonels, majors and adjutants.

Uniform See Plate E.

Royal Police Guard (Guarda Real da Policia) The Royal Police Guard, formed from 10 December 1801 to maintain the internal security of the city of Lisbon as well as to assume garrison duties, was certainly more of a military than a police unit. It consisted of a battalion of infantry and a corps of cavalry, said to have been taken from among the best troops in the army. It had 1,005 infantry and 229 cavalry fit for service in December 1809, and 1,207 rank and file in January 1811. A similar corps, but smaller, was also raised to carry out the same duties in the city of Porto and is mentioned as part of its garrison in 1808.

Uniform See accompanying illustrations and Plate G.

Attached to the police was the Corps of Barrier Guards (Corpo de Guarda Barreira), recruited from older veteran soldiers to act as internal security personnel. They were posted at various roadblocks and kept an eye out for suspicious-looking individuals or goods.

Uniform In 1801: blue coatee with red collar, blue cuffs, blue shoulder straps and turnbacks, scarlet piping, brass buttons, yellow lace buttonholes at cuffs and collar; white or blue pantaloons, black short gaiters; bicorn hat with yellow cockade loop, white-over-black plume. Round hats and red cuffs noted in 1810. Brass-hilted hanger with buff belt and brass oval plate.

Castle Guards (Pé de Castello) This was an old institution going back two hundred years. Although the title was officially changed to companies of Sedentary Garrisons (Guarniçaoes

Officer, Royal Corps of Engineers, 1808-09. This detail from a print after William Bradford, who was in Portugal at the time, shows two rows of gold buttons rather than one, gold lace edging the collar, cuffs and front of the coat, and dark blue collar and cuffs rather than the black of the 1806 regulations. The black must have been mistaken for dark blue by Bradford, but other details are obviously liberties taken by the Portuguese engineer officer (or officers) that he saw. The edging should have been white piping and the coat single-breasted but, with gold lace and two rows of buttons, they were remarkably similar in dress to their British Royal Engineers counterparts, who wore blue faced with black and laced with gold until 1813. The sword is also non-regulation and features a chain guard.

1: Fusilier, Legion of Light Troops, c1805
2: Fusilier, Loyal Lusitanian Legion, 1808-11
3: Fusilier, 2nd Battalion, Loyal Lusitanian Legion, 1809-10

WRY. 2000

A

1: Fusilier, 3rd Cazadores, 1808-09
2: Drummer, 5th Cazadores, c1810-15
3: Fusilier, 6th Cazadores, c1810-15

B

1: Sergeant rifleman, 9th Cazadores, 1811-15
2: Officer, 12th Cazadores, 1811-15
3: Private rifleman, 3rd Cazadores, c1812-13

1: Officer, 4th Cavalry, 1806-10
2: Trumpeter, 11th Cavalry, 1806-10
3: Trooper, 8th Cavalry, 1806-10

D

1: Officer, 5th Cavalry, 1811-15
2: Governor, Garrison Staff, 1806-15
3: Trooper, 10th Cavalry,
   1810-15

WRJ. 2000

E

1: Officer, Royal Corps of Engineers, 1806-15   2: Private, Company of Artificers, 1806-10
3: Officer, Royal Arsenal, c1806-15

F

1: Fusilier, Royal Police Guard, 1804-11
2: Private, Telegraph Corps,
   1810-14
3: Private, Pé de Castelo,
   1806-12

WRY. 99

G

1: Paymaster, Treasury, 1812-15
2: Commissary, Commissariat, 1812-15
3: First Surgeon, Medical Corps, 1806-15

WRY. 99

H

Fixas) in 1762 the old name continued to be widely used. Gunners were especially sought after for this service to maintain and serve the artillery installed in these fortifications. However, such service was probably scarcely known during the Peninsular War; a report of 1809 noted that the majority of the men were peasants and mutilated invalids. They were nevertheless useful, as they freed men fit for service in the field. Each company usually had three officers and a variable number of men. In the province of Estramadura there were 160 men at Setubal, Sesimbra and nearby batteries, 256 in the fortress of Peniche, 273 at Cascais and 227 at Sao Juliao da Barra. In the province of Minho were two companies each of 128 officers and men at Viana and Valenza. Beira had two companies of 128 officers and men. Algarve had 400 men at the batteries of Villa Real and Faro, 260 at Lagos and 140 at Sagres. The Pé de Castello were amalgamated into the new Corps of Veterans (qv) on 2 October 1812.

Uniform See Plate G. The veterans of Alentejo province (Veterano do Alentejo) had a slightly different dress consisting of a blue coatee with blue collar, cuffs, shoulder straps and turnbacks, scarlet collar patch at the front and scarlet piping edging the collar, cuffs, shoulder straps, turnbacks and down the front; brass buttons; white or blue pantaloons, black short gaiters; cylindrical shako with brass band and plate, white plume; brass-hilted hanger with black belt and brass oval plate.

Corps of Veterans (Corpo de Veteranos) Organised from 2 October 1812 by uniting the Pé de Castelo and various other veterans into this new corps. It was made up of veteran soldiers unfit for active service but equal to garrison duties in forts, watchtowers and batteries all over the kingdom. Its companies had up to 120 men including three officers, each province having various numbers of companies; e.g. Alentejo had three but Estramadura had eight. In all the corps had 30 companies gathering 3,600 veterans.

Uniform The dress of the Pé de Castelo continued to be worn but apparently without lapels, the coatee being single-breasted edged with scarlet piping.

Prince's Royal Bodyguard (Guarda Real do Principe) Also called Archers of the Royal Guard (Archeiro do Guarda Real). Unlike other nations, Portugal did not have large guards regiments and this small company was its only true guard unit. A small body of halberdiers, it originated in the reign of King Joao II (1481-95). The term 'archers' denoted their constabulary powers rather than meaning that they carried bows. By the 18th century their duties were entirely ceremonial and the guardsmen were all noblemen at court. They traditionally wore the royal livery of green and white until 1728, when King Joao V assigned them a scarlet uniform with blue cuffs and waistcoats trimmed with gold lace

The Lines of Torres Vedras were not walled fortifications as this mid-19th-century British print might suggest, but actually a maze of mutually supporting forts and batteries taking advantage of the hills north of Lisbon. In 1809-10 tens of thousands of civilians helped by soldiers built some 154 forts armed with 534 cannon and mortars. Secrecy was maintained so that, almost incredibly, the French knew nothing of these formidable works until they stumbled upon them. Marshal Masséna, who could not pierce the lines and anticipated an Anglo-Portuguese attack on his flank and rear out of Peniche, finally retired to Santarem.

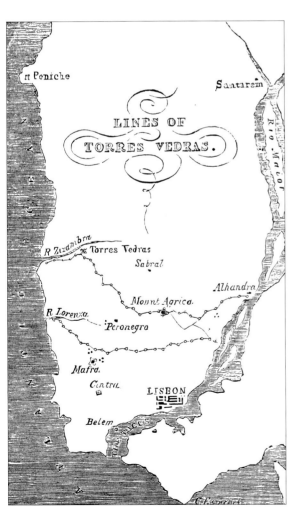

While we cannot be absolutely certain, this French print appears to show a sergeant of the Corps of Artificers, c1815-20. The belt has a buckle like that of the British Sappers and Miners, and the shako plume seems to be black and white. The shako plate seems later and rather fanciful and, by regulation, there should be no buttons on the cuffs. The epaulettes correctly indicate the rank of sergeant.

and buttons. Under Prince Regent Joao VI the company had one captain, one lieutenant, one sergeant, three corporals, a drummer, a fifer and 20 men. They were armed with swords and halberds.

Uniform In full dress they wore a scarlet coat edged and laced at the seams with broad silver lace worked with the royal crest; blue waistcoat laced silver; blue breeches, white stockings and shoes; bicorn hat with a white plume edging and silver lace, and a laced bandoleer. The ordinary uniform was the same except that the lace was gold and plain and that the captain carried a spontoon. The unit left for Brazil with the royal family in November 1807 (see forthcoming MAA 356).

First Plan of the Army (Primero Plano do Exercito) This was a body of noble officers whose origins went back to the Middle Ages when gentlemen at court formed the king's escort. They were said to have been dressed in scarlet, so scarlet became the preferred colour worn by the noble officers in the 18th century. The body of officers was eventually disbanded but its retired members could continue to serve and wear their distinctive scarlet dress at court; it then became the 'Extinct First Plan...' (Extinta Primero Plano) under the 1806 regulations.

Uniform Scarlet coat with scarlet collar and cuffs, yellow piping and turnbacks, gold buttons; bicorn hat, no plume.

Retired Officers (Reformados) Older former regimental officers on the retired list, not formally attached to any unit or corps.

Uniform Blue coat with blue collar, cuffs, piping and turnbacks, gold buttons and epaulettes; bicorn hat with white plume.

CIVIL DEPARTMENTS OF THE ARMY

Treasury of the Army (Thesourarias do Exercito)

This branch of the administration saw to the financial services and combined fiscal auditors, accountants, commissaries and paymasters. One peculiarity which kept them busy was that, in the Portuguese service, officers had no cash allowances for servants or forage as in the British army. Instead they were allowed extra rations and forage in kind, but could convert them to cash if not used. This was 'in fact almost the same thing as the sum of money given to the British officers', according to Halliday; but it must have given rise to a great deal of bureaucratic correspondence between the Portuguese Treasury, Commissariat and 'Vivares' officials. The commissaries were reorganised into the new 'Commissariado' from late 1810 (see below).

Uniform From 1806, a sky blue coat with yellow collar and cuffs, sky blue lapels, scarlet piping and turnbacks, silver buttons and lace, no epaulettes and no plume. The Inspector General had a wide lace edging the coat, a lace edging the collar and cuffs. The Treasurer General had a narrow lace edging the coat, three narrow laces on the cuffs and one on the collar. An Assistant Commissary had the same but two narrow laces on the cuffs. A Commissary Paymaster had no lace edging the coat and a narrow lace edging the collar and cuffs.

This changed on 11 October 1810 to a (dark) blue coat without lapels and with collar, cuffs and turnbacks (and probably piping) of the colour of the division to which the official was attached, with silver buttons, epaulettes and lace. The Treasurer-General had epaulettes with fringes, two silver laces at the cuffs and a narrow silver lace edging the collar and cuffs. An Assistant Commissary had the same except for one lace at the cuffs. A Paymaster of the army in the field had an epaulette with fringes on the right shoulder, one without fringes on the left, and narrow lace edging at collar and cuffs. Commissaries had epaulettes without fringes and a narrow lace edging the collar and cuffs. Subaltern officials had one epaulette without fringes on the right shoulder and one narrow lace at the collar.

On 9 January 1812 the uniform of Treasury officers changed to a blue coat with blue velvet collar and turnbacks, sky blue velvet cuffs, gold lace and epaulettes according to rank, gold buttons marked to the corps; white waistcoat, white or blue pantaloons, plain bicorn hat. The coat was to be as the 1807 undress coat of naval officers (see forthcoming third volume, MAA 356) except for lapels, so it was probably edged with scarlet piping. See Plate H.

'Vivares' and Commissariat

The Portuguese equivalent to the British army's Commissariat was divided into two departments. The Vivares do Exercito was responsible for procuring provisions and food for the troops. It was managed by a Board (or Junta) sitting in Lisbon, with intendants in every province and storekeepers with clerks and subalterns in every major town. They were supposed to maintain adequate stores of supplies but, due to the lack of funds and to various malpractices, this was rarely the case. Peasants were loath to sell supplies to the government since the prices paid were abysmal. Naturally, farmers hid their foodstuffs from the Vivares, and consequently troops might be close to starvation in a town where considerable supplies were hoarded. The army's solution was to send detachments of soldiers to seize supplies by force.

These unsatisfactory methods could work if units were in garrison towns, but everything broke down in wartime when regiments were in the field. The supply officers detached

Cavalry trooper, Royal Police Guard of Lisbon, 1808-09. Blue coatee with scarlet collar, cuffs and turnbacks, yellow lace, brass buttons; white breeches, black boots; black helmet with brass fittings and black plume; buff bandoleer with red central stripe, buff waistbelt, brass buckles, bearskin holster covers. (Print after William Bradford)

with the troops in the field had hardly any money and could only pay with worthless credit notes. The result was that during the 1810 invasion Masséna's troops lived for months on supplies they had found secreted at Santarem, while the Portuguese regiments went without bread for weeks. Wellington and Beresford were not amused.

Marshal Beresford encountered great difficulty in his attempts to reform this branch, which began in earnest from about October 1810. An effective organisation was needed if the Anglo-Portuguese army was to be kept in the field. It was reformed along the lines of the British army's Commissariat with which it now had to work closely. The whole Portuguese structure was put under the command of a Commissary-in-Chief, who henceforth demanded audited purchases at fair prices and payments in cash by subalterns. Commissaries in the field were given roughly the same powers and means as their British counterparts. Gradually, Portuguese (and later Spanish) peasants lost their fear of selling their crops to the army.

The system was, however, far from perfect. The Portuguese treasury was empty. The 1810-11 invasion had ruined thousands of farms in central Portugal, and crops had been destroyed and not replanted; revenue was consequently almost nil and food in limited supply. The Portuguese Commissariat thus had no money to buy what food there was and, to avoid the starvation of the army, Wellington's British Commissariat had to supply large numbers of Portuguese. In late 1812 a damning report attributed a lack of 'discipline of Portuguese troops' to 'privations they suffer ... the spirit of enthusiasm which it was hoped had been combined with the discipline introduced in their army has been very materially affected by the irregularity of payment' together with supply shortages (PRO, WO 1/401). Wellington went so far as to ask the Prince Regent for 'the entire abolition' of the Junta de Vivares, but this was not granted. According to Col Williams, by 'indefatigable exertions, however, these evils, so far as the supplies and reinforcements of the army were concerned, were overcome; and Wellington, in the beginning of May (1813), was prepared to take the field with a much larger and more efficient force' than ever before. However, the Portuguese supply system remained a major problem, causing the desertion of thousands of regular, militia and Ordenanza soldiers who were literally starving.

Wellington was very critical of his own Commissariat, demanding exact and proper services from these Treasury officials in uniform, and he naturally expected the new Portuguese Commissariada to follow suit. Before condemning this body out of hand we should remember that their British counterparts often provided a far from shining example of efficiency and probity – and that a British officer as senior as the Deputy Assistant Commissary-General in the Peninsula was court-martialled and dismissed for embezzlement in 1812.

The Transport Department – Transporte do Exercito – was to provide the means of carrying army supplies. This was generally done by contracting muleteers, carts and barges. It was under the direction of an Intendant-General and 'was generally better managed' although 'defective in many points, and dreadfully expensive', according to Halliday. By 1812-13 Beresford's reforms had increased its efficiency while reducing costs.

Uniform By the 1806 regulations the Vivares officials had a sky blue coat, black collar, sky blue cuffs and lapels, scarlet piping and turnbacks, silver

Infantry fusilier, Royal Police Guard of Lisbon, 1808-09. Blue coatee with scarlet collar, cuffs and turnbacks, yellow lace, brass buttons; blue pantaloons with a yellow stripe, black short gaiters; black 1806 shako with brass plates, yellow cords and black plume; light buff accoutrements, pair of pistols in light buff holster, hanger in black scabbard tipped with brass; Portuguese musket, somewhat shortened, with brass bands and light buff sling. (Detail from a print after William Bradford)

buttons, bicorn hat, no plume. The Transporte officials had the same except for a scarlet collar. Employees of Vivarcs and Transporte had a narrow silver lace edging the collar and cuffs. For Commissariat officers between 1806 and 1812, see Treasury above.

On 9 January 1812 the Commissariat was assigned a blue coat without lapels, with blue velvet collar and turnbacks, scarlet velvet cuffs and probably piping, as it was to be as the undress coat of naval officers except for lapels, with gold epaulettes and embroidery lace according to rank, buttons marked to the corps, white waistcoat, white or blue pantaloons, bicorn hat, no plume. See Plate H.

Medical Services

The Medical Department of the army was headed by a Central Junta in Lisbon made up of the Physician-General and the Surgeon-General who supervised the medical aspects, and the Contador-Fiscal, who was in charge of the treasury and supplies related to hospitals. The medical staff consisted of a First Physician and First Surgeon of the army, physicians and surgeons of brigades and of hospitals, under whom were surgeon-majors, assistant-surgeons and 'infirmieros', who were somewhat like male nurses with medical training. According to Andrew Halliday, one of the British military surgeons in the Portuguese army, the corps was in a deplorable state in spite of attempts to rectify its short-comings before the 1807 invasion. The senior posts were largely sinecures and the various hospital staff neglected their duties, physicians in particular being rarely seen.

Each regiment also had a surgeon-major and two (officially, but Halliday says there were six) assistant-surgeons; however, by Portuguese law they could not perform medical procedures unless approved by the resident district physician, so their actions were much restrained. Another restrictive law prevented them from compounding or mixing drugs, which was the monopoly of apothecaries. The practical result of this well-meaning legislation was that the recovery of a sick soldier was 'left to nature, or the chance succour of some convent', and if he did go to a military hospital 'it rarely happened that he returned to his corps'. In spite of attempts at reform by Dr Abrantes, Inspector-General of Hospitals, who did manage to reduce costs, there was still much left to do when the arrival of the French froze all further activity.

When the army again took the field in 1809 there were 'not ten assistant-surgeons' in it, and even they eventually deserted. Halliday, who was one of the British doctors sent to Portugal, felt that the Portuguese Physician-General and his assistant were 'about a century behind the rest of Europe' in their professional practices, although

Officers of infantry and cavalry, Royal Police Guard of Porto. This print of c1830 shows essentially the uniform worn during the Peninsular War. Both figures have blue coatees and trousers, scarlet collars, cuffs, turnbacks and piping, gold buttons, lace and epaulettes and red sashes. The infantry officer (left) has a shako with gold plates and white-over-red plume, and scarlet-striped trousers. The cavalry officer has a black crested helmet with gilt plates and fittings and white-over-red plume, a red shoulder belt edged with silver, a black sabretache and boots. (Museu Militar do Porto)

Archers of the Prince's Royal Bodyguard, c1806-23. At left, a captain armed with a spontoon, wearing the ordinary uniform with plain gold lace; note the false hair-bag and queue attached to the rear of his collar. The other guardsmen wear the full dress coat embellished with broad silvery lace worked in the national colours which gave a blue and red effect. (Print after J.B.Debret)

he added that this was not the case with many other Portuguese doctors. Indeed, some were actually ahead of the rest of Europe if we are to believe Dr Halliday, who tells us with considerable regret that he 'never knew general blood-letting used as a remedy' by Portuguese doctors.

Beresford obtained the help of 12 British staff surgeons and William Ferguson was named Inspector-General of Hospitals in early 1810. The British medical officers attached to the Portuguese army were 'increased from 12 to 20' in late 1811 (PRO, WO 1/250). They were detached to brigades or attached to Portuguese general hospitals. A considerable supply of hospital bedding, surgical instruments and other medical supplies was sent from England. Appointments were now decided by a qualification board of one British and two Portuguese medical officers, and carried the rank of captain in a regiment. Improvements were made, but physicians stubbornly resisted reforms which were seen as an assault on their professional prerogatives. Beresford needed their co-operation, and relented to the extent that they would not be controlled or ordered by military officers.

The Portuguese medical service had a second establishment of numerous officials and clerks of the Contadoria do Hospitaes, an office set up in the past to prevent abuse of hospital stores and accounts. Over time this had become a somewhat abusive bureaucracy, including Almonxarifes (purveyors), Escrivaos (accountants), Escriptuarios (clerks), Compradors (buyers), Fiels (storekeepers) and many assistants besides. Dr Halliday, as the Portuguese army's Assistant Inspector of Hospitals, was well qualified to state that 'among such a multitude of people, no one knows his proper duties ... and the sick are entirely neglected'.

Uniform From 1806 the medical staff had a sky blue coat, scarlet cuffs, collar, piping and turnbacks, sky blue lapels, silver buttons and lace, bicorn hat, no plume. Surgeons were reminded in May 1807 that they were not to wear smallswords with yellow metal hilts, which was the prerogative of regular officers; theirs were to be of white metal. The Fysico Mor had a narrow lace edging the cuffs and collar with three narrow laces on the cuffs. The Primero Medico and Segundo Medico had respectively three and two narrow laces on the cuffs and one on the collar. A surgeon major had a narrow lace edging the coat, three narrow laces on the cuffs and two on the collar. A first surgeon had no lace edging the coat, three narrow laces on the cuffs and two on the collar. A second surgeon had the same but one narrow lace on the cuffs.

The Contadoria do Hospitaes had the same uniform from 1806 except for a sky blue collar. The Contador General had a narrow lace edging the cuffs and collar with three narrow laces on the cuffs. The 1st, 2nd and 3rd Escrutarios or clerks had respectively three, two and one narrow lace on the cuffs and one on the collar. See also Plate H.

Many civilian doctors and surgeons would also be found treating military personnel in wartime. The traditional dress of the medical profession in Portugal was an all-black suit with a short yellow shoulder cape or mantle.

Police of the Army (Policia do Exercito)

This was an administrative civil department of officials and clerical staff concerned with the administration and procedure of justice in the army.

ABOVE **Infantry colour, mid-18th century. The basic *gyronny* pattern of Portuguese military colours was generally as shown. In 1764 the royal arms were added in the centre. (Print after Pereira de Sales)**

First colour of the 8th Line Infantry, c1810. Yellow saltire cross over red and blue *gyronny* field with the arms of Portugal at centre, regimental designation on scroll, and crowned cipher 'JPR' in gold on white panel at each corner. Reproduction. (Museu Militar do Bussaco)

Second colour of the 19th Line Infantry, c1810. White field with the arms of Portugal at centre, regimental inscriptions on scrolls, and crowned cipher at each corner. Reproduction. (Museu Militar do Bussaco)

Standard of the 3rd Squadron, 5th Cavalry Regiment, c1810: yellow field, natural-coloured coat of arms, gold designation on blue scroll. (Museu Militar do Bussaco)

Uniform Sky blue coat, black collar and cuffs, sky blue lapels, scarlet piping and turnbacks, silver buttons, narrow silver lace edging the collar and cuffs, bicorn hat, no plume.

COLOURS AND STANDARDS

Infantry Colours From the early 1700s each infantry regiment carried a pair of colours. Descriptions are scarce but it seems clear that all colours were of the same design and shades, rather than being distinctive for each regiment as in the British army. The basic design was a field consisting of a heraldic *gyronny* with a border. The triangle and bar patterns were generally green and white up to the 1760s, when they were changed to scarlet and blue. In 1764 the royal arms were ordered added to the centre of the colours. The exception was the Lippe Regiment, organised in 1763, which had colours with a pink field, the royal arms at the centre with a scroll below bearing the name of the regiment, the motto 'Ubi gloria, omne periculum dulce', and the royal cipher at each corner. On 17 December 1795 the regiments that had participated in the Roussillon campaign (1st Porto, 2nd Porto, 1st Olivenza, Peniche, Freire and Cascaes) were allowed to add to their colours the inscription 'Ao Valor do Regimento do...' followed by the name of the unit.

The 19 May 1806 regulations specified that each regiment had a pair of colours. The First Colour consisted of a complicated pattern of 16 blue and scarlet 'quarters' split into triangles and border bars, over which was superimposed a yellow saltire cross with the royal arms at the centre on a white circle, and below this a blue scroll with the regimental designation in yellow letters. The crowned yellow cipher 'JPR' (Joao Princepe Regente) in a white square was displayed in each corner. The Second Colour was much plainer, having the field in the colour of the regiment's military division (white, scarlet or yellow as indicated by the regimental piping and turnbacks), with the arms of Portugal in the centre, the regimental designation on a scroll, and the crowned cipher at each corner. A silk sash was tied in a bow below the finials of both colour staffs, in the colours of the regimental collars and cuffs.

Artillery Colours There is no information on artillery colours before the May 1806 regulations, which specified that each regiment had a pair of colours which were similar in design to those of infantry regiments. It is assumed that this was also the case before 1806.

ABOVE **Special honorary colour granted to the 7th and 11th Cazadores in 1813. Blue and red *gyronny* field like line infantry first colours but without the yellow saltire or the scroll with regimental designation; below the royal arms is a bouquet of green palms wrapped in a white scroll bearing '*Dinstintos vos sereis na lus historia – Com o louros que colhestes na Victoria*'. The cords were blue and scarlet, as was the sash tied in a bow below the spearhead finial.**

ABOVE RIGHT **First colour of the 9th Line Infantry, c1814. Similar to that of the 8th, it has an additional white commemorative circlet around the coat of arms, bearing in yellow lettering '*Julqareis qual e mais existente: se sr do mundo rei se de tal gente*'. The 9th, 11th, 12th and 23rd Infantry were awarded this circlet for exceptional service. The scroll below is blue with yellow lettering.**

Cazadores Colours The Cazadores battalions did not carry colours, except for the 7th and 11th towards the end of the war. On 13 December 1813 the 7th and 11th Cazadores were each allowed an honorary colour as a mark of their distinguished service, especially at the battle of Vittoria. These were of the pre-1806 design without the yellow saltire (see illustration).

Militia Colours By the 1806 regulations each militia regiment was to have a pair of colours of the same design as those of the regular infantry. The First Colour was blue, white, scarlet and yellow. The Second Colour was of the colour of the regiment's uniform lining (see forthcoming MAA 356). The sash below the finial was in the colour of the regimental collars and cuffs.

Cavalry Standards Each cavalry regiment had one standard per squadron. The standards were square and, from the early 1760s, appear to have had the royal arms at the centre; the colours are unknown. By the 1806 regulations all standards had the same design but the colour varied according to the squadron: the 1st Squadron was white, the 2nd scarlet, the 3rd yellow and the 4th blue. Each standard had the royal arms at the centre and above a blue scroll with the regimental designation in yellow. The silk sash below the finial was in the colour of the regimental collars and cuffs.

Other units and flags The Royal Police Guard infantry and cavalry had colours and standards marked with 'Guarda Real da Policia – Vigilancia e Seguranca'. The Lisbon Royal Commerce Volunteers raised from December 1808 (see forthcoming MAA 356) had a pair of colours for the infantry and four cavalry standards; design was according to the 1806 regulations, with a scroll bearing 'Patriotismo e Fidelidade' above the royal arms and 'Voluntarios Rais do Comercio' below. The national flag of Portugal was white with the royal arms at the centre.

IN FRENCH SERVICE

La Légion Portugaise

From 16 January 1808 three numbered line regiments and two cavalry regiments were formed from part of the disbanded Portuguese army.

On 20 February a 3rd Cavalry and 4th and 5th Infantry regiments and a battalion of light infantry were ordered formed, the light unit from the remnants of the Legion of Light Troops (qv). This new Portuguese army in French service was put under the command of the Marquis of Alorna, who was given general's rank. On 21 March 1808 Napoleon ordered all Portuguese troops 'formed or not' – about 8,000 men – to march out of Portugal through Spain to Bayonne and Languedoc in southern France. Some elements remained with the French army in Spain, notably the light infantry battalion at the first siege of Zaragoza, but it was thought wiser to reorganise the Portuguese army in France, further from home. On 18 May this command was renamed as a legion within the Grande Armée, to be formed in southern France. The Portuguese Legion was to have six light infantry regiments of six companies of 140 men each; and two regiments of mounted chasseurs having four squadrons, each with two companies of 100 men. All elements were gathered at Grenoble and Gray during that summer, but only five infantry regiments could be formed by August. In March 1809 a temporary '13th Elite Provisional Half-Brigade' was formed from the Legion's grenadier and voltigeur companies, and fought with distinction at Wagram (5-6 July). By the time the rest of the Legion reached Austria the campaign was over, and it returned to its depot at Grenoble.

On 2 May 1811 the establishment was again reduced, no doubt for lack of recruits, to three infantry regiments and one regiment of mounted chasseurs. In June 1812 the whole Legion marched into Russia, its regiments dispersed between various corps. They fought at Krasnoe (14 August), Smolensk (17 August), Polotsk (18 August) and Borodino (7 September); but most of the Legion was lost in the disastrous winter retreat. In April 1813 there remained 965 officers and men including 131 cavalrymen. The cavalry was disbanded and all survivors were mustered into a temporary depot battalion. Grumbling and desertion increased; on 8 October 1813 the troops were disarmed, and on 25 November the Portuguese Legion was formally disbanded. The men were not released from service but were to be formed into a pioneer battalion (see below).

Uniform The initial regiments formed in January and February 1808 kept their blue Portuguese uniforms, the decrees stating that new facing colours would later be assigned. They never were; and by May Napoleon had decided that the Portuguese Legion's uniform would be brown instead of blue – see illustrations.

The mounted chasseurs also had a brown coatee with scarlet collar, cuffs, lapels and turnbacks, white piping, pewter buttons and scarlet wings; grey-blue cavalry trousers with scarlet stripe, black boots; black leather helmet with black caterpillar crest, scarlet plume; white sheepskin housings edged red. Trumpeters had reversed colours with yellow wings having white lace and fringes, and white plumes. From 1812 the troopers had a brown single-breasted coatee with scarlet collar, pointed cuffs,

turnbacks and piping, pewter buttons; brown breeches laced white or brown overalls with a scarlet stripe to each side. The helmet was discarded for a French-style shako with brass plate and chinscales, white cords and green pompon. The elite companies had a fur busby with red bag piped white. Officers initially had gold buttons and epaulettes, and a red waist sash with silver tassels as in the Portuguese service. From 1812 they had silver buttons and epaulettes and no longer wore a sash.

Pionniers Portugais Pioneer battalion of four companies raised from men of the disbanded Legion from 25 November 1813; sent to Bourges and disbanded 27 April 1814, the men to return to Portugal.

Uniform The unarmed pioneer battalions were to wear a light grey-blue single-breasted round jacket with light grey-blue cloth-covered buttons, light grey-blue waistcoat, pantaloons, forage cap, short gaiters and greatcoat with brass buttons, shako with brass plate and chinscales.

* * *

The epilogue was bitter for the survivors of the Legion. They knew they were renegades in their countrymen's eyes, and might be treated as traitors if they returned home – indeed, some few who had started for Portugal had been compelled to turn back when roughly handled in Spain. Now refugees in France, some joined the Régiment Colonial Étranger; this was a unit raised by Louis XVIII on 16 December 1814 to give the Portuguese and Spaniards in the former Imperial service a chance to serve as colonial troops safely stationed overseas. Napoleon came back before they had been shipped to the colonies. The colonial regiment was disbanded on 2 May 1815; its men were used to form the 6th Foreign Regiment at Tours, but it was still being organised when Napoleon was defeated at Waterloo. King Louis XVIII was restored and, on 6 September, Napoleon's foreign regiments were disbanded. Four officers and some of the remaining men joined a new foreign regiment, while 65 other ranks retired in France. The Marquis de Alorna was never again to see his lovely family estate near Santarem.

THE PLATES

A1: Fusilier, Legion of Light Troops, c1805
In about 1803-05 the uniform of the Legion changed and became more stylish. The infantry were clothed with a sky blue coatee with a black collar, cuffs and turnbacks, three rows of brass buttons on the chest connected by flat yellow lace, two laces at the collar, two on the cuff and two above on the lower sleeve; yellow lace edged the facings. They received both white gaiter-trousers and sky blue breeches, with black gaiters. The black 'stovepipe'-style shako was embellished with yellow cord and a white plume on the left side, but no shako plate. The uniform remained the same under the 1806 uniform regulations except for the shako plume, which was changed to green. (Museu Militar, Lisbon)

A2: Fusilier, Loyal Lusitanian Legion, 1808-11
The Legion's infantry wore a green coatee with green collar, pointed cuffs and shoulder straps, and three rows of pewter buttons in front; white lace edged the collar, cuffs, front, turnbacks and shoulder straps, and the latter had white fringes. Green pantaloons were worn in winter and white in summer. The shako had a brass oval plate and a pointed lower band bearing a triple 'L'; a green plume rose from the national cockade in front. There were 48 drummers and 12 buglers equipped with 'bugle horns' garnished with 'bugle cords'. The chasseurs were armed with British muskets, most likely of the India Pattern, except for 120 riflemen who had rifles – surely Bakers – with black rifle accoutrements. The artillery had black collars and cuffs. Four French brass 4-pounders and two 5½in howitzers complete with travelling carriages were sent from Britain to Portugal in 1808, obviously meant for the artillery company. One was destroyed in battle at Alcantara in May 1809 and the five remaining pieces were probably attached to one of the artillery regiments in later 1809. The light cavalry was to have green faced with white collars and cuffs. (Museu Militar do Porto; PRO, WO 6/172)

A3: Fusilier, 2nd Battalion, Loyal Lusitanian Legion, 1809-10
This figure is based on an inspection report of January 1810 which found the battalion deficient in many respects. The men were said to be 'in different kinds of clothing ... some green, grey & mostly worn out', with white summer trousers. This indicates that some of the grey jackets sent to Portugal in 1809 were issued to the Legion. The accoutrements were 'Portuguese large pouches' with 'black belts'; the arms were British, and serviceable in both battalions. (PRO, WO 1/244)

B1: Fusilier, 3rd Cazadores, 1808-09
This unit was apparently the first to be fairly well uniformed and armed from the time of its raising in late 1808. This jacket has previously been interpreted as having wide flat yellow buttonhole lace (which would translate as 'galao') ending in a point on the chest. However, the original order mentions

'cordao amarello' – yellow cord. Indeed, apart from its colours and the shako the general style of the uniform was obviously influenced by the dress of the Loyal Lusitanian Legion. The yellow cords (gold for officers) and buttons were not especially practical and were changed to black from July 1809. The 3rd had dark brown collars and yellow cuffs until 30 July 1811. (1808 regulations; PRO, WO 1/232)

B2: Drummer, 5th Cazadores, c1810-15
Musicians had regimental uniforms with distinctive lace edging the collar and cuffs. Drum-majors, drummers and fifers had green and white lace, buglers had green and yellow. The drum case was brown, the jacket colour, painted with a simple crowned 'JPR' cipher; the hoops were probably painted black from 1809. The 5th had scarlet collars and cuffs. (Museu Militar, Lisbon)

B3: Fusilier, 6th Cazadores, c1810-15
This was the standard dress worn by the Cazadores during their campaigns with Wellington which took them from Portugal to France. While many Cazadores were armed with Baker rifles, about two-thirds of each battalion were armed with India Pattern smoothbore muskets and had black accoutrements. The 6th had yellow collars and cuffs; the battalion was raised in Porto and was part of the renowned Porto Brigade which served with distinction in Wellington's army. This unit was present at all major battles and was more fortunate than most others, as it suffered only 97 killed and 195 wounded during the war. (Museu Militar do Porto)

Private's coatee, 6th Cazadores Battalion, c1811-15. Brown coatee with yellow collar and cuffs, black cords and lace and black metal buttons, brown shoulder straps edged with black lace and fringes. (Museu Militar do Porto)

C1: Sergeant rifleman, 9th Cazadores, 1811-15

Cazadores NCOs adopted the British-style chevrons of rank in black, which Marshal Beresford allowed them to wear instead of the rank badges of the Portuguese 1806 regulations. This sergeant has three chevrons, is armed with a Baker rifle and carries its accoutrements. The 9th, formed in 1811 from the Loyal Lusitanian Legion, was distinguished by scarlet collars and black cuffs. It saw much action right up to Toulouse in April 1814, suffering 411 casualties of all ranks including 139 killed. (Ordem de Dia, 30 July 1811 and 24 March 1813)

C2: Officer, 12th Cazadores, 1811-15

The officers' jacket was trimmed with black silk cord from 1809. We show the epaulettes which were the regulation rank distinction. However, a system of laces made official in 1815 may have been previously used from about 1813 in some units. The 12th had scarlet collars and sky blue cuffs. Although not at full strength the battalion was reported by Dr Halliday to be 'in excellent order'. At the battle of Salamanca the 12th distinguished itself by taking a French Eagle, which LtCol Crookshanks 'delivered to General Pack on the field of battle' (Halliday).

C3: Private rifleman, 3rd Cazadores, c1812-13

This figure is based on a painting by Dennis Dighton in the Royal Collection, showing a rifleman in a simplified jacket without cords but with black collar and cuffs. These match the 3rd Battalion's facings from 30 July 1811 (although Dighton's subject is often taken to be of the 4th Cazadores because of the numeral '4' on the shako on the ground nearby). This jacket had the three rows of black buttons without the complicated braiding across the chest, similar to the standard jacket style worn by British rifle units; this may possibly have been an undress allowed by its commander, LtCol George Elder, detached from the 95th Rifles, but it was not the official battalion uniform. Dighton also shows the pantaloons to be grey rather than brown. The 3rd was part of the British Light Division and was often mentioned in despatches by Wellington for its gallant conduct. It suffered some 439 casualties including 160 killed during the war.

D1: Officer, 4th Cavalry, 1806-10

Officers had the same uniform as their men but of better quality materials, with gold epaulettes and crimson sash with silver tassels. The 4th had scarlet collars and cuffs with white piping and turnbacks. The regiment was raised in 1762 as Mecklemburg and numbered 4th in 1806. It fought in many actions between 1809 and 1814. (All three figures are based on the 1806 regulations.)

D2: Trumpeter, 11th Cavalry, 1806-10

Cavalry trumpeters had the same uniform as the men of their regiment except that their jackets were trimmed with yellow lace at the seams. The trumpet-major had yellow silk lace and sergeant's epaulettes. The 11th had sky blue collars and cuffs with scarlet piping and turnbacks. The regiment was raised as the Almeida Cavalry in 1715. Numbered 11th in 1806, it was present at most major battles and many small engagements between 1808 and 1814.

D3: Trooper, 8th Cavalry, 1806-10

The new 1806 uniform was dark blue with, for the 8th, yellow collar and cuffs with scarlet piping and turnbacks. The regiment fought a number of actions in south-eastern Spain during 1810-11.

E1: Officer, 5th Cavalry, 1811-15

In November 1811 uniforms with some 539 'caps (shakos) & tufts with oiled covers, scales, plates, &c', plus '1 Beaver Do. Do. for Sergeant Major' were sent to the 5th Cavalry from England. The 5th had scarlet collars, cuffs, piping and turnbacks. This uniform was rendered by Dighton in 1812 with, however, the shako bearing the numeral '10'; our figure is based on the painting but with '5' on the shako. The regiment was raised as the Evora Dragoons in 1715, officially designated cavalry and numbered 5th in 1806. (PRO, WO 1/849)

E2: Governor, Garrison Staff, 1806-15

Officers of the Estado Maior de Praza wore a blue coat with black collar and cuffs, blue lapels, scarlet piping and turnbacks, gold buttons and epaulettes; red sash with silver

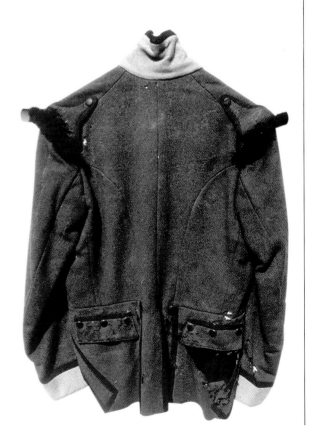

Back view of the 6th Cazadores coatee. This is an original garment, but has suffered various restorations over the last hundred years. The brown shoulder straps edged with black lace and black fringes appear to have been made smaller from previously salvaged material; the originals would have been larger. Note the three vertical lengths of black lace at the rear of the skirt, on the central seam and the flanking seams; and the horizontal black lace on the pocket flaps. (Museu Militar do Porto)

tassels; bicorn hat laced gold with mixed scarlet, blue and gold tassels, and yellow and black plume; and carried a gilt-hilted smallsword. A governor below the rank of general officer wore the garrison staff uniform with seven gold buttonhole laces on each lapel, as illustrated. Epaulettes were as for line officers. A governor having the rank of general wore his general's uniform. (1806 regulations)

E3: Trooper, 10th Cavalry, 1810-15
The 10th is one of the regiments known to have received shakos from Britain in 1810. Illustrations and prints show the

shakos as wider at the top than the bottom and generally similar to the British 1812 light dragoon type. Dighton shows a black shako with the numeral '10' and the chinscales in yellow metal. The pointed brass band stamped with the regimental number (or name) at the bottom and the brass oval national plate appear to have been adopted later. The 10th had sky blue collars and cuffs with white piping and turnbacks. The metal shoulder straps continued to be used into the 1830s. (PRO, T 28/9)

F1: Officer, Royal Corps of Engineers, 1806-15
From 1806 the uniform of the corps was a blue coat with black collar and cuffs, white turnbacks, white piping edging the coat front, collar and cuffs, gold buttons stamped with a castle, and gold epaulettes; white breeches in summer and blue in winter; red sash with silver tassels; black boots; bicorn hat laced gold with mixed blue, black and gold tassels, and a white and black plume. (1806 regulations)

F2: Private, Company of Artificers, 1806-10
From 1806 the uniform was a blue coatee with blue collar and cuffs piped scarlet, black lapels piped scarlet, scarlet turnbacks and piping on skirt and blue shoulder straps, and white metal buttons; blue or white pantaloons and black gaiters. The *barretina* shako had a white metal bottom band with black letters 'ARCM', a shako plate or badge consisting of crossed axes in white metal, white cords, and a red-over-black plume. The officers wore the same colours but had long tailed coats, silver buttons and epaulettes, red sash, and a bicorn with a silver loop but no plume. (Arquivo Historico Militar, uniform album K)

F3: Officer, Royal Arsenal, c1806-15
The uniform of the specialist military officers working at the Royal Arsenal consisted of a blue coat with blue collar and cuffs, yellow piping, white turnbacks, gold buttons and epaulettes; red sash with silver tassels; white breeches, black boots; and a bicorn hat with black plume. (Arquivo Historico Militar, uniform album K)

G1: Fusilier, Royal Police Guard, 1804-11
Its first uniform when raised in December 1801 was a blue coatee with scarlet collar, cuffs and lapels which closed from neck to waist, blue lining, yellow metal buttons, yellow buttonhole lace; brown breeches in winter and white in summer, and a black leather helmet. In 1804 the lapels were discontinued, the coatee becoming single-breasted with laced buttonholes; the turnbacks changed to scarlet. It was worn with blue breeches and black gaiters. The headgear changed to a shako with brass plates, yellow cords and a black plume – this was the *barretina* shako introduced in the army two years later. The British-style 'stovepipe' shako was probably adopted around 1810-11.

G2: Private, Telegraph Corps, 1810-14
The corps' uniform was a blue coatee with blue cuffs, shoulder straps and turnbacks and a black collar; white

Lieutenant Bernardo de Sa Nogeira, 4th Cavalry Regiment, c1806-10. The 4th had a blue coatee with scarlet collar and cuffs, white piping and turnbacks. (Print after portrait)

piping edged the collar, cuffs, shoulder straps, turnbacks and the front, and buttons were brass. White or blue pantaloons were worn with black short gaiters. The cylindrical shako had a brass band and plate, and a white-over-black plume. The sidearm was a brass-hilted hanger on a buff belt with a brass oval plate. (Arquivo Historico Militar, uniform album K)

G3: Private, Pé de Castelo, 1806-12

The uniform of these veterans' companies was a blue coatee with blue collar, cuffs, lapels, shoulder straps and turnbacks, scarlet piping and brass buttons; white or blue pantaloons and black short gaiters; and a shako with brass band and plate and a black-over-red plume. A brass-hilted hanger was worn from a buff belt with a brass oval plate. The lapels may have been omitted from c1811. (1806 regulations; Arquivo Historico Militar, uniform album K)

H1: Paymaster, Treasury, 1812-15

From 1810 the rank of paymaster was distinguished by an epaulette with fringes on the right shoulder, one without fringes on the left and narrow lace edging at the collar and cuffs. In January 1812 the Treasury adopted a blue uniform with sky blue cuffs and changed from silver to gold buttons and lace. (Arquivo Historico Militar, Uniformes, caixa 5)

H2: Commissary, Commissariat, 1812-15

From 1810 ordinary commissaries were distinguished by epaulettes without fringes and a narrow lace edging the collar and cuffs. The blue uniform with scarlet cuffs was introduced in January 1812, when the silver button colour changed to gold. (Arquivo Historico Militar, Uniformes, caixa 5)

H3: First Surgeon, Medical Corps, 1806-15

Medical Corps personnel who served in the military hospitals had basically the same uniform from 1806 to 1815: a sky blue coat with scarlet cuffs, collar, piping and turnbacks, sky blue lapels, silver buttons and lace and a plain bicorn hat. A first surgeon had three narrow laces on the cuffs and two on the collar. (1806 regulations)

Captain, Royal Corps of Engineers, campaign uniform, c1802. Blue coat, black velvet collar and cuffs, scarlet turnbacks, gold buttons, blue shoulder straps edged scarlet; crimson sash with silver tassels; blue breeches, black boots; black round hat with black plume; gilt-hilted sword with crimson sword knot and silver tassels. (Anne S.K.Brown Military Collection, Brown University)

RIGHT **Gold buttons and lace from the January 1812 uniform regulation for Treasury and Commissariat: (I) Treasury, (II) Commissariat, (III) embroidery lace pattern for the Treasurer General and the Assistant Commissary. These senior officials had one such lace at each side of the collar and three to each cuff. The Commissary Paymaster had laces on the cuffs only.**

INDEX

COMPANION SERIES FROM OSPREY

CAMPAIGN

Concise, authoritative accounts of history's decisive military encounters. Each 96-page book contains over 90 illustrations including maps, orders of battle, colour plates, and three-dimensional battle maps.

WARRIOR

Definitive analysis of the appearance, weapons, equipment, tactics, character and conditions of service of the individual fighting man throughout history. Each 64-page book includes full-colour uniform studies in close detail, and sectional artwork of the soldier's equipment.

NEW VANGUARD

Comprehensive histories of the design, development and operational use of the world's armoured vehicles and artillery. Each 48-page book contains eight pages of full-colour artwork including a detailed cutaway.

ORDER OF BATTLE

The most detailed information ever published on the units which fought history's great battles. Each 96-page book contains comprehensive organisation diagrams supported by ultra-detailed colour maps. Each title also includes a large fold-out base map.

ELITE

Detailed information on the organisation, appearance and fighting record of the world's most famous military bodies. This series of 64-page books, each containing some 50 photographs and diagrams and 12 full-colour plates, will broaden in scope to cover personalities, significant military techniques, and other aspects of the history of warfare which demand a comprehensive illustrated treatment.

AIRCRAFT OF THE ACES

Focuses exclusively on the elite pilots of major air campaigns, and includes unique interviews with surviving aces sourced specifically for each volume. Each 96-page volume contains up to 40 specially commissioned artworks, unit listings, new scale plans and the best archival photography available.

COMBAT AIRCRAFT

Technical information from the world's leading aviation writers on the century's most significant military aircraft. Each 96-page volume contains up to 40 specially commissioned artworks, unit listings, new scale plans and the best archival photography available.